BABES in the WOODS

Hiking | Camping | Boating
with Babies & Young Children

Jennifer Aist

To children everywhere:
may they each delight in experiencing the joy of nature

THE MOUNTAINEERS BOOKS
is the nonprofit publishing arm of The Mountaineers,
an organization founded in 1906 and dedicated to the exploration,
preservation, and enjoyment of outdoor and wilderness areas.

1001 SW Klickitat Way, Suite 201, Seattle, WA 98134
© 2010 by Jennifer Aist
All rights reserved
First edition: first printing 2010, second printing 2013, third printing 2015
No part of this book may be reproduced in any form, or by any electronic, mechanical, or other means, without permission in writing from the publisher.
Distributed in the United Kingdom by Cordee, www.cordee.co.uk
Manufactured in the United States of America

Copy Editor: Kris Fulsaas
Cover and Book Design: Ani Rucki
Layout: Ani Rucki

Cover photograph: © Brad Mitchell/Alamy

Library of Congress Cataloging-in-Publication Data
Aist, Jennifer.
   Babes in the woods : hiking, camping, boating with babies & young children / Jennifer Aist. — 1st ed.
      p.   cm.
   Includes bibliographical references and index.
   ISBN 978-1-59485-343-2 (ppb)
   1. Outdoor recreation for children. 2. Family recreation. I. Title.
   GV191.63.A57 2010
   796.5083—dc22
                        2009051823

ISBN (paperback): 978-1-59485-343-2
ISBN (e-book): 978-1-59485-344-9

CONTENTS

INTRODUCTION

"What do parents owe their young that is more important than a warm and trusting connection to the Earth . . .?"
—Theodore Roszark, *The Voice of the Earth*

Babies in the backcountry? Absolutely. With a lifelong love of being in the outdoors, I couldn't wait to plan a backpacking trip with my first baby. She was about four months old and had already traveled on many an Alaskan trail. But what about bears? What about bugs? What if the baby gets sick or hurt? What if it rains the whole time? I knew how to handle these situations for myself, but somehow with a baby in tow everything I knew about camping needed to be reevaluated.

With many unanswered questions, I packed up and headed out. No one got sick; no one was injured. It didn't rain. The bugs were a hassle, but overall we had a fabulous time, and I was hooked. I couldn't wait to start planning the next adventure.

Through the years, our family has experienced a lot of rain, a broken arm or two, sick kids, sick moms, and occasionally some cranky moods. But more than anything, we've had tons of smiles and four kids who truly love and respect the backcountry as much as my husband and I do.

In the beginning, I had a ton of questions. How do you keep a six-month-old entertained on your back for a four-hour hike? What do you really need to bring for a weekend camping trip? What if someone gets sick or injured? What if the baby won't sleep in a tent? How do you keep little ones warm and dry?

I scoured the Internet and read every book I could find on camping with children. What I found was a lot of information about camping with older children and barely more than a page or two on babies. There was a lot of information about weekend RV camping but next to nothing on tent camping with toddlers in the midst of potty training. So I kept hiking with my family, improvising as we went, and I started keeping notes and taking pictures. Before I knew it, I had amassed a whole lot of information on taking babies and toddlers into the backcountry. Other families I knew went on their own adventures and came back to share their experiences.

Meanwhile, more and more people were asking for advice about taking their children out in the woods. At the request of many families, in 1999 the first "Babes

Sometimes the smallest things in nature bring children the most pleasure. [LARISSA WRIGHT-ELSON]

in the Woods" class was held at the Children's Hospital at Providence in Anchorage, Alaska; by the second year, we filled an auditorium with people coming from all over to learn the tricks and tips my family and others had accumulated through the years. I now teach annual "Babes in the Woods," "Babes in the Snow," and "Babes on the Water" classes—all of which are well attended by families excited to share the outdoors with their young children.

During the past ten years, the interest of families in taking their very young children out camping has increased exponentially. Today's parents tend to incorporate parenting into their regular lives rather than put aside their favorite activities to stay home with babies. Camping and hiking are activities no longer reserved for those considered hardcore. More and more people are taking an interest in wild places and, thus, a desire to share those places with their children. Families are also finding that travel costs are keeping them closer to home on vacations. Camping is the perfect eco- and budget-friendly vacation.

The camping industry has responded by creating better gear and clothing designed for infants, toddlers, and preschoolers. Personal flotation devices (PFDs) are now

Big smiles today make for happy memories forever. [JEN AIST]

available for newborns. Jogging strollers are now considered basic baby equipment. Clothing manufacturers even make wool socks and clothing out of polypropylene—a tough-as-nails, quick-drying material—for newborns. The Resources section gives you an idea of where to find the amazing gear available now.

This book is intended not only to inspire families to adventure with their young children but also to educate them so they have a safe and meaningful experience. The information is the product of miles and miles of time on trails with my four children either in my belly, on my back, or on my heels. Perhaps more importantly, it is a product of many families learning to camp and returning home to share their expertise. From their travels and my own, I have learned hundreds of tips and tricks to make the wilderness more accessible for you and your kids. You'll feel equipped to plan a short day hike, a car camping trip, a base camping adventure, a boating excursion, or a backpacking trip in spring, summer, or fall in a variety of climates. See the Checklists section for easy-to-use reminders of gear to bring.

This book uses the following age categories:
- **young infants:** birth to six months
- **older infants:** six to fifteen months
- **toddlers:** fifteen months to three years
- **preschoolers:** three to five years

The benefits of connecting children and adults alike with nature are far-reaching. A 1997 study of preschool children in Norway and Sweden compared motor development outcomes of groups of children who played on either typical flat playgrounds or in natural settings with uneven ground. After one year, the children who played in natural settings tested better for motor fitness, in particular balance and agility. It is truly a new development of the last 100 years that we don't spend the majority of the day outdoors on uneven ground in varying weather conditions.

Our physiology is much more adapted to outdoors than it is to climate-controlled indoor environments. Our immune system is challenged by breathing recycled air riddled with viruses and bacteria from heating and ventilation systems. Our bone mass is decreasing due to lack of weight-bearing exercise. (Weight bearing on bones increases bone mass and, in turn, bone strength.) Elevators, escalators, moving sidewalks, and other modern marvels have eased our commutes and daily tasks, but the price has been high, as evidenced by alarming increases in levels of obesity. We need to get back outside and get moving.

American families have shifted from spending all of their time outside to being afraid to go outside at all with their children. I hear so many parents telling me their fears about taking young children out hiking—even for day hikes. They are afraid of the weather, getting lost, catching colds, and the thousands of "what ifs" that loom over parents. The fact is, you can't catch a cold from being cold or wet; very few children get lost in the woods; and, most importantly, babies and young children are incredibly resilient. In reality, your baby is at far greater risk when riding with you in a car on the highway than when riding on your back down the trail.

The balance between modern technology and nature has shifted too far. We as parents have the opportunity to shift the balance back for our children. Our babies and children are well suited for the great outdoors. So are we. We don't need to forgo modern technology or our minivans; we just need to reincorporate nature into our lives. It is my most sincere hope that this book will help more and more families begin a tradition of sharing our great back-

This mother and son are ready for adventure.
[LARA BROCK]

country with their children. If we can do that for our babies, we will be giving them, and perhaps our planet, the greatest gift.

I look forward to seeing you on the trail!

PART I

Taking Care of the Basics

Clothing | Food | Sun | Bugs | Dirt | Sleep | Safety

CLOTHING

"Some people walk in the rain; others just get wet."

—Roger Miller

Y ou may have heard the admonition "There's no such thing as bad weather—just bad clothing." Clothing children for the outdoors may take a bit of know-how and some creativity, but with the right gear, you need not let cold, wet, or even very hot weather stop you from taking your children outside. Once you know the basics, you'll be ready to take on just about any kind of weather.

WET AND COLD WEATHER

Knowing how many layers to put on ourselves in cold weather is easy. Knowing when your three-month-old baby is warm enough is another issue. With young babies or children who are sitting still or being transported, the easiest way to check is to feel the child's core body temperature. Simply stick your hand on your child's bare chest or armpit. If he or she is sweaty, take off a layer; if the skin feels cool, add a layer. Feeling cheeks or hands won't tell you if your child is dressed appropriately; these areas often feel cool even when the body is plenty warm. Children who are actively moving on the trail are generating their own heat, so you will likely need to be on the lookout for overheating rather than chilling.

ESSENTIAL GEAR CHECK
Wet- and Cold-Weather Clothing

- wool, silk, or polypro base layer
- fleece or wool insulating layer
- rain suit (top and bottom or one-piece) outer layer
- hat and mittens
- wool socks, plus an extra pair
- rain boots or water shoes

Should your baby ever get really cold, here are some simple tricks to warm him or her up. First, get your baby skin-to-skin against you and bundle up all around. Your body heat will warm your baby. For anyone older than one year, the single most effective way to generate heat is to move. When your kids tell you they are cold, get up and take them on a jog, start dancing with them, or wrestle in the tent. Movement generates heat; clothing insulates and keeps it in.

Base Layer

Think of dressing kids as being similar to frosting a cake (hint: your child is the cake!). Before your cake is perfectly frosted, you'll need a good crumb coat or base layer. This is a critical moisture-wicking layer that keeps skin dry.

Avoid cotton as a base layer. When cotton gets wet, it stays wet and chills the body. Fabrics of choice in wet and cold conditions are wool, silk, and polypro. (Polypropylene is a synthetic material that dries quickly and wicks away moisture from the skin.)

Many clothing manufacturers list their base layers in terms of weight. Mid-weight and expedition-weight are the thickest. You'll want both long-sleeved tops and full-length bottoms.

Wool and synthetic materials will protect this little guy from getting cold in case he gets wet.
[TOM TWIGG]

Start collecting clothing for this base layer now. Get on hand-me-down lists, shop garage sales or online secondhand sites, or buy new. More and more companies like Patagonia and Molehill are making outstanding performance layers for babies, toddlers, and young kids. While you might cringe at the price tags at first, remember that quality gear will last through several children, and there is a big resale market for these items. Quality gear is worth the expense. Quality base layers keep kids warm. Warm kids are happy kids. Happy kids make happy parents. Happy kids and parents make for a great trip!

TIPS & TRICKS

Start looking for gear in your own closet. Here's how to modify adult-sized layers to fit babies:
- **Leg warmers 1.** Cut the sleeves off old long-sleeved wool or synthetic shirts to fit baby legs nicely.
- **Leg warmers 2.** Cut the toes off old wool socks then slide the socks onto your baby's legs to add a warm base layer.

Your baby's new ensemble may look a bit rough, but luckily it isn't a fashion show out there!

We camped one weekend in the pouring rain. The kids got totally soaked. They poured water out of their boots by the cupfuls, and their rain suits proved practically worthless, soaking every layer we put on them. But their bodies were warm. Their feet were warm. Why? They were wearing all-wool socks and all-polypro layers under their raincoats. Because of that, we were able to stay and play, and by the next morning, most of their clothes had dried in the tent.

Insulating Layer

After the base layer, depending on the temperature, your child may need to add a warm layer such as a fleece shirt, fleece vest, or wool pullover. While individual needs certainly vary, most children will need an extra layer when it is windy or the outside temperature dips below 60 degrees F. (Think of this as your first full-on frosting layer.) Wool and polyester fleece are your best fabric choices.

Outer Layer

For the final "frosting" coat or outer layer, your child needs a raincoat. Quality raingear is really important. Most of the PVC (polyvinyl chloride) plastic or vinyl raingear found at discount stores will not hold up to foul weather or rough play on the trail. The plastic material cracks and leaks rain onto layers beneath. Plastic and vinyl also don't breathe at all, so active kids get really sweaty and wet under their rain suits even if the rain doesn't leak through. It is usually cheaper in the long run to invest in mid- or high-quality raingear in the first place.

Look for items made with Gore-Tex or a similar waterproof-breathable fabric. I don't like the rain jackets with fleece lining because they take forever to dry, are heavy, and are not very packable. And the shells are often made from nonbreathable PVC plastic or vinyl.

For babies and pre-potty-trained toddlers, look for one-piece rain suits that have cuffs that flip into mitts and fit over their hands and feet. This style provides better coverage for ever-moving youngsters who like to jump, splash, crawl, roll, and sit in puddles or other bodies of water. The downside to one-piece suits is that they usually don't provide easy access for diaper changing. (There's always a trade-off!) Here are some keys to picking a good one-piece rain suit:

- Make sure the hood has some sort of bill on it to shed water away from the baby's face.
- It should be lightweight and easy to pack into a small nook of your pack.
- Buy big. Some companies make one-piece suits up to size 4T. You'll get more mileage out of a bigger suit, and you can always roll up the sleeves and legs. Having some extra room in the suit will also allow your baby to wear extra layers under it. The longer pants are also less likely to ride up when you are carrying your baby in a carrier. The smallest suit I ever bought was the 18-months size.

For older toddlers, preschoolers, and beyond, you have three options:

1. One-piece suit
2. Bib overalls with a jacket
3. Pants with a jacket

Toileting with either of the first two options is a bit of a hassle, especially during potty training and when it's cold or rainy (though boys have a bit of an advantage). You are buying the suit to keep them dry, though, not for ease of toileting.

One-piece rain suits work better on babies than two-piece ones. [KJERSTIN THOMAS]

Footwear

Footwear for kids who will be in cold and wet conditions is like the flowers on the frosted cake. Most folks use rain boots, which are readily available and inexpensive in the spring. A good sole is nice for durability, and handles make them easier to pull on, but otherwise, a rain boot is a rain boot. However, despite all your efforts, rain boots will get full of water. This will undoubtedly lead you to wonder why you brought them in the first place, and so more and more I *don't*. But some parents really like them.

If you're expecting some snow on the trail, bring gaiters (which seal the boundary between pant cuffs and boot tops) to help keep shoes and pants dry. If there is going to be substantial snow, bring snow boots.

TIPS & TRICKS

Adult wool socks can be pulled on over toddler or preschool shoes to add some insulation and turn ordinary shoes into cold-weather boots.

On some trips, I bring water shoes: shoes with closed toes and heels that are often made of mesh and neoprene (a synthetic rubber used in wetsuits) with sturdy soles. If the temperatures are on the cool to cold side, I have the kids wear wool socks with the water shoes. Open-toed sandals pose a risk for toes getting hurt.

Make sure that whatever footwear your child is wearing isn't too tight. With babies, it is easy to overtighten booties with shock cords. Always test the elastic to make sure you can easily get a couple of fingers between the elastic and your baby. One mom told me that she had booties on her six-month-old daughter, and the baby kept crying and crying, but her mom couldn't figure out what was wrong. Finally, Mom stripped her baby down to check her out head to toe. It turned out the elastic cording of her booties was so tight on her ankle that there was a deep mark all the way around it. Once the booties were off, the baby stopped crying!

Beware of any footwear with shock cords or long loops hanging off the top. These can get caught on obstacles and trip children. Either choose a different brand or cut off the cords. Don't risk unnecessary falls.

Finally, bring plenty of socks. Always have an extra pair in your pack, even on day hikes and totally blue-sky days. Young children will always find water and will always step in it. Warm, dry socks can really improve everyone's mood. Wool socks are your best bet. These are available in all sizes, including newborn. You could even knit socks for your kids. Avoid cotton socks.

Headgear and Handwear

Heat loss occurs from any exposed area of the body, so cover up those little heads and hands. A fleece jacket's hood works, although a hat is more effective. Hoods tend to leave gaps around the face, whereas hats provide better coverage.

Mittens are warmer than gloves and much easier to put on little hands. For toddlers, I recommend mittens without thumbs.

Adding an extra layer like a hat can keep everyone on the trail happier. [TOM TWIGG]

WILD FACT
Heat Loss

You lose approximately 7 percent of your body heat through your scalp. Bald heads do not lose any more heat than hairy heads. When you are hypothermic and shivering, the amount of heat lost through your scalp increases to 55 percent but returns to 7 percent once you have warmed up some.

HOT AND HUMID WEATHER

Dressing for hot and humid environments is more like giving your cake a light glaze or just a dusting of powdered sugar, to continue our cake analogy. Parents tend to strip the baby down to just a diaper, but this isn't always the best decision. For one thing, it puts the baby at major risk of sunburn. It also doesn't keep the body any cooler.

Base Layer

Dress babies and young children in loose-fitting garments made of tightly woven materials, preferably with a high ultraviolet protection factor (UPF) rating (see the Sun chapter). Avoid tank tops or shirts with straps. Long-sleeved shirts are best. Tight-fitting sun shirts or rash-guard shirts made of synthetic materials like spandex don't perform well at keeping you cool in high-humidity areas such as the tropics and the southeastern United States. They are great in dry heat and block ultraviolet radiation well, but they tend to cling to your body in high humidity. This can lead to rubbing, chafing, and rashes, in addition to interfering with the body's natural ability to cool itself via sweating. Cotton T-shirts are a poor choice due to cotton's habit of hanging onto sweat and not allowing evaporation. If your journey takes you through humid climes, try a naturally wicking material such as linen or a loose-fitting sun shirt.

Pants or a long, loose dress is best for a bottom layer. In addition to keeping your child cooler, long pants also provide much-needed protection on the trail. Naked ankles are open to bug bites and at risk for scrapes and cuts from brush and rocks on the trail. Long pants can go a long way in protecting little legs.

Headgear

Hats are a critical layer in sun protection for your child. Wide-brimmed hats work best. Baseball caps alone do not provide adequate coverage unless you

ESSENTIAL GEAR CHECK

Hot- and Humid-Weather Clothing

- UPF-treated, loose-fitting shirt and pants
- lightweight windbreaker in case temperatures drop
- hat with wide brim
- lightweight wool socks
- closed-toe and -heel sandals

use a bandanna underneath it. (See the Sun chapter for more information about sunhats.) The hat should shade the child's face, ears, and neck. Consider bringing along an umbrella to provide added shade.

Footwear

Finding shoes and socks for hot environments isn't always easy. Many children's shoes, especially waterproof ones, are very hot to wear and don't breathe. Look for a shoe with a lot of airflow on the sides and good toe protection. Thin wool socks will protect feet from developing blisters on hikes but aren't necessary if the child will be carried most of the time.

Simple precautions like sunhats will go far in protecting young skin. [LEN MATERMAN]

Outer Layer

Desert areas that can reach past 100 degrees F during the day can drop down to near freezing at night. Make sure you have appropriate layers to put on as the temperature drops.

A packable (can be scrunched up tightly and shoved into tiny pockets in your pack) wind or rain shell makes a perfect outer layer. The shell will help retain heat and keep the wind from chilling the child.

WATER SPORTS

Dressing for water sports necessitates some special clothing. Water can be dangerously cold even in hot climates. Your children's safety depends on clothing that will protect them in the event of a submersion. Cotton won't cut it. Make it a practice to wear only wool, silk, nylon, or polypro on the water.

A wind or rain shell makes a perfect outer layer that helps retain heat and keeps the wind from chilling the kids.

No matter your vessel, keep a dry bag (a specially constructed waterproof gear bag) full of extra layers, including a hat, mittens, warm socks, tops, and bottoms in case anyone goes in the water. It is also a good idea to bring a sleeping bag stored in a dry bag on trips—even day ones.

Most river guides will tell you that

Match the clothing to the activity: a sun shirt provides great protection for this young child playing in the sun. [LEN MATERMAN]

the majority of injuries happen to feet, and they happen in camp. So make it a rule that your child must always wear something on his or her feet. What that is depends on the types of beaches and boats you will be on. Rain boots are fine for flat, sandy beaches. However, rubber rain boots can be clumsy and slippery for kids on rocky beaches with seaweed. For these locations, use a shoe that supports their feet and has some traction underneath it. Look for a water shoe that has closed toes and heels and will dry quickly.

ESSENTIAL GEAR CHECK
Water-Sports Clothing

- wool, silk, nylon, or polypro layers
- personal flotation device (PFD) with a whistle
- wind or rain shell
- thicker dry layers packed in a dry bag for emergencies
- water shoes, rain boots, or sandals

SAFETY TIP

Consider dry layers part of your safety kit.

FOOD

Co-written with Kendra Twigg

"One of the very nicest things about life is the way we must regularly stop whatever it is we are doing and devote our attention to eating."

—Luciano Pavarotti and William Wright, *My Own Story*

When you're camping, meals can either make or break the trip. With kids, this is doubly true. Not only are good meals essential for satisfying hunger and making everyone feel good, but they are also vital for providing essential nutrients and energy necessary for playing hard, having fun, and staying warm in the great outdoors.

TEMPTATION NUMBER 1: SKIMPING ON FOOD

When planning a camping trip, often the need to simplify can lead to the temptation to short-change our children and ourselves on the necessary calories and nutrients needed to stay safe and warm. Don't yield to this temptation. When camping, it is important to pay attention to some basic nutritional guidelines. In fact, what we choose to eat can very much be a safety issue.

Playing out in the great outdoors burns a lot of calories. With all the hiking, climbing, exploring, tree climbing, and general running around that kids do, they will need to eat more, not less, than at home. How much more will vary according to air temperatures, activity levels, kids' size, and the individual metabolism of each child. So how do you figure it out for meal planning? And how do you ensure they are getting enough if they eat only a few bites—and this applies particularly to toddlers—at a time?

1. Anticipate larger meal portions than normal.
2. Have snacks available throughout the day.

Look at all foods, especially snacks, as important opportunities to provide valuable nutrition . . . not just calories to fill kids up temporarily. Besides offering a variety of nutrients such as vitamins and minerals, food offers us energy in the form of calories. Different foods offer different caloric densities.

When you're camping in warm or temperate climes, eat a little more than your normal diet, with several healthy snacks to provide your child with plenty of calories.

When you're in colder temperatures and/or expending a much greater amount of energy than usual, ensure that the foods and snacks you offer are denser in calories: choose nuts over pretzels if your child is older than three years (nuts are a big allergen that should be avoided earlier on), and add fats such as butter, oil, cheese, and seeds to meals. The colder the temperatures, the more calorie-dense your meals need to be.

TEMPTATION NUMBER 2: CONVENIENCE FOODS

Another temptation when trying to plan quick and easy-to-cook meals is to select prepared or convenience foods. The problem with this is that many of these foods are highly processed and high in simple carbohydrates and low in complex carbohydrates and protein.

A common analogy is that foods are fuel for the body, just as wood is fuel for a fire. Not all wood burns the same; just as different sizes and densities of wood burn differently, different foods provide different levels and durations of energy for the body.

Simple carbohydrates, such as sugars and refined grain products (cookies, crackers, white bread products) are your kindling. Like small dry grasses and twigs that burn easily, they burn fast and furious. It would require a great amount of kindling to keep a fire going on that alone, so when we need more than a quick boost we turn to other fuels.

Complex carbohydrates (whole grains) are your sticks. They both take longer to burn and provide some good immediate energy that is sustainable for a longer period of time.

Proteins and fats (meats, tofu, eggs, peanut butter) are your logs. Not only necessary for kids' growth and development, they also provide long, continuous burning to maintain energy and the body's core temperature.

A convenience diet of prepared foods provides doses of kindling, which burn out midway through the day and leave campers feeling tired and lethargic. With kids, this can present itself as a total meltdown . . . or, in other words, unhappy campers who will make everyone else miserable. Which isn't so convenient, after all.

WATER, THE OTHER NUTRIENT

While we typically give a lot of thought to what food we eat, the same usually isn't true about the water we drink. Think about what you'll carry drinking water in; bisphenol A (BPA), which has been linked to Type 2 diabetes, angina, coronary heart disease, and heart attacks, is present in many plastic containers. Stainless-steel or other non-BPA-containing water bottles are a good option; another is a water-bladder system.

Never is your water consumption more apparent than when you have to carry it on your back, pump it through a filter, or haul it back to camp. When preparing for your trip, it is vital that you think about how much water you will need to drink, cook with, and clean with. You need to know if there will be safe water sources at the campsite, if you will have to bring it all with you, or if you will need to purify it on-site.

Purifying Water

It is so important to have clean water for young children. Much of the earth's surface water is unsafe to drink because it is contaminated by surface runoff containing human or animal feces or other contaminants. Even in wilderness settings where there has been little human impact, the risk of contracting an illness from bacteria, viruses, or protozoa is significant if you drink untreated water. For this reason, you should be familiar with water treatment methods. It is recommended that in addition to your primary water treatment system, you also plan on a back-up or secondary system in case your primary system fails. Here's the lowdown on the treatment methods available:

Boiling water at a rolling boil for at least one minute (three minutes at higher elevations) is a highly effective means of destroying bacteria, viruses, and protozoa cysts. But boiling uses a lot of fuel, takes time, and can give water a "flat" taste.

Filters force water through a porous material that prevents particles from passing through. Look for a filter that can remove particles as small as 0.2 micron. Most commercially available filters remove bacteria and protozoa but do not remove viruses, so research whether viruses are a concern in the area where you'll be drawing water.

Chemical treatments are available in the form of iodine or chlorine drops or tablets. They kill bacteria and viruses, as well as some—but not all—protozoa, but they aren't recommended for young children or pregnant women. They're lightweight and compact, but they can take time with cold or cloudy water, and they leave a disagreeable taste.

UV light has been used to purify water on a larger scale for some time now, but it has only recently become available as a personal portable method suitable for camping and backpacking. These devices use UV light to sterilize water in a very short time (less than one minute for a pint), destroying 99.99 percent of viruses, protozoa, and bacteria. They are powered by batteries and turn themselves off after each sterilization cycle. They are not as effective with water containing particulate matter (which must be prefiltered). You can purchase a prefilter or buy a model that includes a prefilter, or simply filter water through cloth prior to treatment with UV light. Because it is battery dependent, always pack extra batteries or bring a small solar power attachment.

Getting Your Babes to Drink

Encourage children to drink water throughout the day, both by letting them take small hydration sips on the go as well as by taking more formal "snack and sip" breaks. Pay attention to how much they are drinking so that you can encourage them to drink more if you feel they need it. Infants younger than three months do not need water at all (see "Baby Milk and Baby Food" later in this chapter). Make it fun to drink water. Figure out games or little tricks to get them to drink. Here are a few favorites:

Encourage little ones to drink often. [CARA HOGGARD]

- Call out group drinks: "One, two, three . . . everybody drink!"
- Have them try to throw a pebble into a circle drawn in the dirt and take a swig for every miss . . . or bull's-eye, depending on how good they are.
- When you stop to take a drink, talk about it: "I'm really getting thirsty . . . a drink of water sounds good about now . . . maybe I will have a sip."
- "Ah . . . that was good; it felt so good on my dry throat."

Do not think of water as something you offer kids only on camping trips. Make it a part of your everyday life. You cannot expect your children to suddenly start drinking water if they are used to drinking only juice, soda, or milk at home. I usually offer my children water throughout the day and milk or juice only at mealtimes. We take water bottles with us on car trips, whether long or short.

If your child just won't drink plain water, you may have to offer fluids in different forms. I am not a huge fan of flavored drinks, but camping necessitates some special exceptions, especially if it gets an otherwise reluctant drinker to drink.

Several healthy powdered drink mixtures are available, but be cautious of drinks with vitamins and minerals. Most contain 1,000 mg of vitamin C as well as other minerals and different combinations of vitamins. Too high a vitamin intake can be hazardous or toxic for children, especially fat-soluble vitamins A, E, and K; they are not flushed from the body as readily and can accumulate in the organs to toxic levels. Read all ingredients when deciding on a product with supplements, and consider other sources your kids may be ingesting the same day, such as energy bars and other snacks or vitamin supplements.

TIPS & TRICKS

A method of sprucing up drinking water is to simply add a splash of fresh lemon or lime juice. Pack an actual fruit to slice as you go, or take a plastic squeeze bottle. You can also purchase dehydrated lemon or lime juice in either bulk or individual packets. Or lightly flavor drinking water by dissolving hard candy, such as a Jolly Rancher or Life Saver, right in the water bottle. Hard candies are easy to pack, and the effect is much like slightly watery Kool-Aid . . . yet still pretty tasty.

Drinking in Cold Weather

We all know how difficult it can be to stay hydrated when camping in hot, dry weather, but it is easy to overlook how cool or rainy weather can dampen our desire to drink. Offering hot drinks can really make a difference not only in providing some necessary hydration but also in warming and cheering up the crowd.

For this reason, a large thermos is standard equipment on most of my trips (except, perhaps, on backpacking trips). When filled in the morning, it can provide a welcome hot drink break later in the day when kids and grown-ups alike need a quick warm-up.

Flavored water is just as tasty hot. In addition, hot cider, hot tea, and hot instant soups are good options. Hot chocolate is an all-time camping favorite that should always be included; just be aware that it doesn't provide as optimal hydration as "clear" drinks do.

MEAL PLANNING 101

There is no single best approach to meal planning for camping. Instead, a plethora of choices allow for customization to your own needs and desires. But it can also be very confusing, especially if you're new to camping. Start by asking yourself a few questions:

ESSENTIAL GEAR CHECK
Drinking Water

- personal water containers
- purification system
- large water container in camp (optional)
- thermos in cold weather

What Type of Camping Will You Be Doing?

Car camping or base camping? Backpacking or boating? Obviously, car camping affords quite a few more options not only about the food you bring but also the equipment you'll use to cook it with. Base camping, especially if you will not be breaking camp every day and packing all your supplies to the next spot, can be very much like car camping. Kayaking or boating limits how much you can carry by volume, but weight is not as much a factor. Backpacking, obviously, limits the amount of cookware as well as food that you can carry.

How Big Will Your Group Be?

Will it be just you and your kids? Will you have extended family or friends joining you? A group of several families? Planning for just your own family can be simple and straightforward. You know what your kids like, you know how much they eat, and you have ultimate control.

Car camping allows simple luxuries such as plenty of dishes and a vinyl tablecloth for a clean space to eat. [MICHELLE WAGNER]

For larger groups, you can expect meal planning to be a bit more complicated, but you have several choices. You can have a food coordinator who does it all (as on a guided trip), from planning to buying to packing. Some people really like to do all the prep, so if you are one of them, go for it.

You can also have a team of people (say, one adult from each family) get together to prepare everything. Or you can divide responsibilities: one or more people plan meals and make a shopping list, one or more people do the shopping, one or more people pack the food.

Another option is to have each family provide a day of meals; some coordination is prudent to make sure there is good variety and everyone is aware of allergies and strong dislikes. Or have each family share a dinner, while each family brings their own breakfast, lunch, and snacks.

Of course, there is nothing wrong with each family planning all their meals separately. As a group, you need to decide what will work best and what equipment will need to be brought, shared and otherwise.

A screen tent makes a perfect bug-free zone for this multifamily breakfast. [JEN AIST]

What Kind of Weather Are You Likely to Experience?

Cold weather calls for more food and for foods that will provide long-lasting energy and warmth. Hot drinks and soups are important. Hot weather will dictate more juicy fruit and salty snacks.

What Is Your Style?

Do you like to linger around the campfire preparing a gourmet meal? Or are you a minimalist who just wants to eat and get going? Obviously, your type of trip will dictate how much time you have for meal prep, but personal style is also an important factor.

The bottom line is, serve what your kids will eat. A camping trip is no place to spring new foods or recipes on them. Choose meals that are normal foods for your family and that adapt well to camping. Save new recipes for when you're home.

I have camped with my kids in hot, arid climates, in the ever-changing weather of Alaska and the Pacific Northwest, and in wintery, snowy conditions. I have backpacked with just my own kids; I have car camped as a single family; I have "taken over" a campground with ten or more families; and I have gone on extended wilderness base-camp kayaking trips with multiple families. Each of these situations presents unique challenges to meal planning and execution. Some tried and true recipes are suitable for all types of trips, but mostly there is a lot of careful thought and endless list-making and packing that makes it all happen, no matter what the situation. Some questions that will be determined by your personal style are these:

- What kind of cook stove will you need?
- How much fuel will you need?
- Will you need a frying pan?
- Will you need a large boiling pot?
- What kind of seasonings should you bring?
- How much cooking oil will you need?

PACKING THE KITCHEN GEAR

Use the general guidelines in the chart in Checklists at the back of the book to help you decide what kitchen gear you should bring. Customizing your own list for cooking gear, kitchen gear, cleanup gear, and eating utensils will make packing much easier.

ESSENTIAL GEAR CHECK
Kitchen Gear

- camp stove or fire, fuel, lighter
- pots, pans, bowls
- cooking utensils
- kitchen shelter, table, chairs (optional)
- cooler or food storage system
- washtub, biodegradable soap
- eating utensils, plates, bowls, cups

CHOOSING THE FOODS TO BRING

Before delving into recipe suggestions, here are some of my favorite camp food tips.

Quick-cooking pastas (orzo, cappellini) are usually a big hit with little kids. Couscous and bulgur wheat are also popular. Quinoa is easy to transport, is healthy, and cooks quickly. Rice is easy to cook, but it can take a long time and a lot of fuel, especially brown rice. Try rice that is already cooked in the pouch or instant rice, which cooks in half the time.

It's possible to have fresh eggs when you're camping, but they should be consumed the first or second day. They make good additions to ramen, or they can be boiled, scrambled, or fried for a breakfast wrap. Some folks bring them already hard boiled. Most pediatricians advise that babies avoid eggs until they are one year old.

Dried Foods

Backpack cooking is usually best kept simple and straightforward. You are limited in what you can carry due to weight, volume, and lack of refrigeration. But simple to prepare does not necessarily mean bland or boring. Think about bringing dehydrated foods. With some ingenuity and perhaps some advance preparation, you and your family can enjoy some tasty meals on the trail.

Jonathan has taken his children backpacking since they were small babes. He

Father and son enjoy a nice bagel by the sea. [JENNY MILLER]

makes all of his meals ahead of time and dehydrates them himself. He advises experimenting with this at home, because some meals dehydrate better than others. He dries his spaghetti sauce, pasta, chicken, veggies—everything! Jonathan finds that the weight is reduced substantially and his meal options expand exponentially.

TIPS & TRICKS

To dehydrate your own meals, cook them as normal then spread the cooked food on a baking sheet. Put it in the oven at about 125 degrees F and check it in an hour or so. Most ovens can be set no lower than 225 degrees F, so you'll have to play around with how far open the oven door needs to be to bring it down to a low temperature.

You can dry your food yourself or purchase a food dehydrator. Jonathan recommends buying one with opaque sides, because light degrades the nutritional value of dehydrated foods quickly. Dried meals can be stored in labeled resealable plastic bags in the freezer.

You can also purchase ready-to-prepare dehydrated meals. All you need to do to cook any of these meals is to add hot water. Instant soup flakes from bulk bins—such as split pea or lentil—are easy options as well. Instant soup packs can add flavor to any meal or be cooked as soup alone.

No-Fail Recipes

The following charts show some tried and true camp meals. Quantities are approximate, per person per day, and should be tested and personalized. Some meals require multiple ingredients, described under Notes or in a separate entry.

Fresh-picked blueberries stirred into pancake batter makes a fabulous breakfast treat. [JEN AIST]

NO-FAIL RECIPES

D=Day Trip | C=Car Camping | B=Base Camping | P=Paddle Sports | S=Sailing | BP=Backpacking

BREAKFAST	QUANTITY	TRIP TYPE	NOTES
Hot cereal (oatmeal, multigrains, kashi, cream of wheat, etc.)	½ cup per person; 1–2 packets per person	C, B, P, S, BP	Instant oatmeal packets are convenient, but the whole grain is much healthier, has less sugar, and creates less garbage. Other hot cereals work well too. Consider stirring in raisins, craisins, seeds, or nuts.
Couscous	½ cup per person	C, B, P, S, BP	For a superquick breakfast, it can be soaked the night before.
Dry cereal and milk	1 cup cereal per person; ½ cup milk per person	C, B	Try to limit sugary cereals, which have a lot of empty carbs. Granola comes in many varieties. Powdered or canned milk can be substituted for fresh.
Dried fruit	¼ cup per person	C, B, P, S, BP	Try bananas, apples, pears, peaches, apricots, mango, and pineapple for variety.
Canned fruit	½ cup per person	C, B, P, S	Avoid individual-sized cans to reduce garbage.
Bacon, sausage	1 pound for 3–4 people	C, B, P, S	Beware: be very careful cooking bacon or sausage in bear country.
Eggs	1 per person	C, B, P, S, BP	Eat in the first couple days: scrambled, hard-boiled, omelets, etc.
Yogurt	1 cup per person	C, B, P, S	Try stirring in some granola or dried fruit for added yummies.
Breakfast burrito	½ per child, 1 per adult	C, S, BP	These can be prepared just like you do at home, with tortillas, scrambled eggs, salsa, and anything else you like to add.
Pancakes	1 per child, 3 per adult	C, B, P, S, BP	Bring a mix that needs only water added for ease of use. Condiments include butter, syrup, jam, et cetera. Try including fresh-picked berries for a special treat.
LUNCH	QUANTITY	TRIP TYPE	NOTES
Peanut butter or cream cheese and jelly sandwiches	½ per toddler, 1 per preschooler, 2 per adult	D, C, B, P, S, BP	Bagels, tortillas, and pitas all make good bread; regular sandwich bread tends to get smooshed unless you're car camping. Individual packets of cream cheese and jelly are good for backpacking.
Cheese sandwiches (plain or grilled)	1 per child, 2 per adult	D, C, B, P, S, BP	Any bread and any cheese will work. Harder cheeses last longer on backpacking trips.

LUNCH, cont.	QUANTITY	TRIP TYPE	NOTES
Tuna fish, egg salad, or chicken salad sandwiches	½ per toddler, 1 per preschooler, 2 per adult	D, C, B, P, S, BP	Tuna in pouches and individual mayo packets make a hearty trail meal. Be careful to clean the tuna smell out of the pouch. Canned tuna or chicken works well when weight isn't as limited.
Bagel with melted pepper jack cheese	½ per kid, 1 per adult	D, C, B, P, S, BP	One of our favorite backpacking meals. Slice the cheese and place it in a nonstick pot, then place the bagel on top. Keep twisting the bagel to keep the cheese from sticking.
Ramen noodle soup	½ pack per preschooler	D, C, B, P, S, BP	This is good, quick, emergency food to have for a cold day. Hard-boiled egg can be added for extra protein. Other instant soups work well too.
Dinner leftovers	1 cup per kid, 2 cups per adult	C, B, P, S, BP	Store in resealable plastic bags for a quick lunch the next day.

POWER SNACKS	QUANTITY	TRIP TYPE	NOTES
Pepperoni or salami	¼ cup per person	D, C, B, P, S, BP	Presliced makes a quick, convenient, no-mess snack.
Jerky	1–2 ounces per person	D, C, B, P, S, BP	Whether turkey or beef, pay attention to the sodium levels. Great emergency food.
Sliced cheese	½ pound per 3 people	D, C, B, P, S, BP	Wrapped in foil, cheese can stay fresh for 2–4 days in moderate temperatures.
Walnuts, almonds, cashews, peanuts	½ pound per adult	D, C, B, P, S, BP	*No* nuts for children younger than three.
Sunflower seeds and raisins, craisins, or dried cherries	¼ pound per person	D, C, B, P, S, BP	Experiment to find your family's favorite combination.
Yogurt raisins	¼ pound per person	D, C, B, P, S, BP	Beware: these make a huge mess in hot weather!
Trail mix, sweet or salty	½ cup per person	D, C, B, P, S, BP	Remember: *no* nuts for children younger than three.
Granola, nutrition, or breakfast bars	1–2 per person	D, C, B, P, S, BP	The soft ones are hard to keep from getting smooshed.

POWER SNACKS, cont.	QUANTITY	TRIP TYPE	NOTES
Baby carrots	¼ pound per person	D, C, B, P, S, BP	Eat early on backpacking trips to lessen the weight. Steam them for toddlers and infants to reduce the choking hazard. Provide some nut butter for extra calories for kids older than three.
Apples, oranges, etc.	1 per person	D, C, B, P, S	Bring softer fruit only if you can store it without smooshing it.
Bananas	1 per person	D, C, B, P, S, BP	Great for babes. You can purchase a special case to pack your fruit in so it won't get smooshed.
Freeze-dried fruit	¼ cup per person	D, C, B, P, S, BP	This is super lightweight, great for babies and older kids alike. Note: freeze-dried is different from dehydrated.
Fruit leather	2 sticks per person	D, C, B, P, S, BP	Be careful to brush children's teeth well after they eat dried fruit. It really sticks to teeth.
Crackers, pilot bread	3–6 per person	D, C, B, P, S, BP	These store well in tall, skinny water bottles.
S'mores	1–2 per person	D, C, B, P, S, BP	While graham crackers, toasted marshmallows, and chocolate are not a power snack, they are powerfully fun.
DINNER	**QUANTITY**	**TRIP TYPE**	**NOTES**
Soft Tacos	1 per kid, 2 per adult	C, B, P, S	Tacos are great for any trip where you'll have a cooler to store perishables.
Tortillas	1 per kid, 2 per adult		Spinach or tomato tortillas have extra flavor.
Ground turkey	1 lb per 4 people		Cook meat with taco seasoning at home to save time.
Refried beans	1 12-oz can per 4 people		A vegetarian option; add taco seasoning.
Taco seasoning	¼ cup per 4 people		Choose one your kids like.
Shredded cheese	½ pound		Save time by shredding cheese at home. (You can use it to make cheese quesadillas as well.)
Chips	½ bag per 4 people		Pack chips with other items you don't want crushed, like bread.
Salsa	1 cup per 4 people		Store fresh salsa in a cooler; store jarred salsa in a cooler after opening.

DINNER, cont.	QUANTITY	TRIP TYPE	NOTES
Sour cream	½–1 cup per 4 people		Store in a cooler at all times.
Guacamole	1 cup per 2 people		Bring some avocados and make it fresh; otherwise store prepared guacamole in a cooler.
Pesto Pasta with Chicken		C, B, P, S	Cook the pasta, then toss with pesto, parmesan cheese, pine nuts, tomatoes, and chicken.
Spaghetti noodles	1 lb per 5 people		You can vary the shape of the pasta too.
Pesto mix	1 6-oz packet of instant pesto seasoning per pound of pasta		Bringing fresh pesto sauce will save you a pot or bowl to wash.
Olive oil	¼ cup per pound of pasta.		Store in a small plastic bottle to prevent spills. Skip the olive oil if you use ready-made pesto and/or don't add oil to the pasta water.
Parmesan cheese	1 cup per 5 people		Bring already grated parmesan for easy assembly.
Pine nuts	1 cup per 5 people		
Sun-dried tomatoes	1 6-oz jar per 5 people		These offer color, flavor, and a kick of vitamin C.
Frozen, ready-cooked chicken or canned chicken	1½ pounds per 5 people		Do not bring raw chicken unless you cook it the first night. Heat up canned or pouch chicken instead. Apple-chicken sausage is also good; sauté it in olive oil before adding it.
Hot Dogs or Hamburgers	1 per kid, 2 per adult	C, B, P	This is an easy, kid-friendly meal to have on every menu.
Hot dogs	1 per kid, 2 per adult		You can use tofu, chicken, beef, or any type of dog. Roast over a campfire or heat on a stove.
Hamburger patties	1 per kid, 2 per adult		Shape and freeze them at home for easiest preparation in camp, then cook on your camp stove.
Hot dog or hamburger buns	1 per kid, 2 per adult		Choose whole wheat for added nutrition.
Ketchup, mustard, relish	¼ cup each per 4 people		Other condiments could include lettuce, tomato, onions, and pickles. Bring your favorites.

DINNER, cont.	QUANTITY	TRIP TYPE	NOTES
Chicken and Rice Soup		C, B, P, BP	This is an easy one-pot meal. Add enough water to almost fill your pot, bring it to a boil, then stir in the bouillon and other ingredients.
Chicken bouillon	6 cubes per 4–6 people		Add bouillon to taste: 1 bouillon cube = 1 cup of broth.
Canned or pouch chicken	1 12-oz can or pouch per 4–6 people		If backpacking, use chicken in a pouch to reduce weight and trash.
Rice	1 lb cooked per 4–6 people		Try ready-cooked brown rice with peas and carrots, or cook the rice at home to save time and cooking fuel in camp.
Carrots	2 per 4–6 people		Peel and cut up the carrots. Dehydrated carrots (or other vegetables) work great.
Peas	¼ cup per 4–6 people		You can add any veggies; these are just the most kid friendly.
Sloppy Joes		C, B, P	This is a messy but tasty meal.
Canned sloppy joe mix	2 12-oz cans per 4–6 people		Heat the mix. Feel free to add beans if you like.
Hamburger buns	½ per toddler, 1 per big kid or adult		Use whole wheat for added nutrition. Tortillas, bagels, or sandwich bread can be substituted.
Grated cheese	2 cups per 4–6 people		Save time by grating cheese at home.
Chicken Pot Pie		C, B, P, BP	Bring the soup to a boil, add chicken and veggies, then drop spoonfuls of prepared biscuit mix on top of the soup and cover the pot. The steam will cook the biscuits like dumplings.
Canned chicken soup or chicken bouillon	2 12-oz cans or 4 cubes bouillon for 4 people		Aim for a thick soup. Pick your favorite.
Pouch or canned chicken	1 12-oz can or pouch per 4 people		If you are backpacking, use the pouch pack to reduce weight and trash volume.
Mixed veggies	½–1 cup for 4 people		Use your favorite combination. Most kids love carrots and peas.
Instant biscuit mix	1 cup for 4 people		Mix with water in a bowl per package directions.

DINNER, cont.	QUANTITY	TRIP TYPE	NOTES
Taco Salad		C, B, P	Combine all ingredients in a large resealable plastic bag, shake, and serve.
Ground beef or turkey	1 lb meat per 4 people		Cook meat at home with taco seasoning to save time.
Taco seasoning	¼ cup per 4 people		Use a mixed seasoning the kids will like. If the adults want it spicier, bring along some extra spices.
Shredded lettuce	1 head per 4 people		
Olives, tomatoes, kidney beans	per personal taste		Bring your favorite condiments in quantities to suit your family.
Grated cheese	2 cups per 4 people		Save time by grating cheese at home.
French dressing	⅔ cup per 4 people		Bottled dressing works fine, or make your own ahead of time. Add enough dressing to cover the salad well.
DRINKS	**QUANTITY**	**TRIP TYPE**	**NOTES**
Water	1–2 quarts per person per day	D, C, B, P, S, BP	Always bring a treatment method with you.
Hot cocoa	1 packet per person per day	D, C, B, P, S, BP	You can create your own mix with powdered milk, cocoa, and sugar.
Hot cider	1 packet per person per day	D, C, B, P, S, BP	If space allows, bring a thermos to fill with hot water at camp. This way, a hot drink is always easy to prepare.
Coffee and tea	1–2 servings per person per day	D, C, B, P, S, BP	Teabags are easier to deal with than loose-leaf teas.
Jolly Rancher or Life Saver to flavor water	1 pack per trip	D, C, B, P, S, BP	Choking hazard: remove the candy or make sure it is all dissolved before giving flavored water to a child.
Instant lemonade or orange drink	1–2 servings per person per day	D, C, B, P, S, BP	Tastes great hot, too!
Electrolyte-type drink	1 per person per day	D, C, B, P, S, BP	Don't drink more than one per day due to vitamin content.

Baby Milk and Baby Food

Breastfed babies need only bring their moms along for their milk. Many moms delay weaning by a summer to take full advantage of this huge convenience. Breastfeeding also offers site-specific immunity, which means the baby is protected from any bacteria, viruses, and protozoa that the mother touches or is otherwise exposed to. This is especially important when the water supply is sketchy. So if the mother is exposed to *giardia,* her body will build antibodies to the *giardia* and pass them onto her baby. This won't provide 100 percent protection from the baby getting giardiasis, but it will lessen the symptoms. (Pretty cool, isn't it?)

ESSENTIAL GEAR CHECK
Food
- breakfasts
- lunches
- power snacks
- dinners
- hot and cold drinks
- baby formula, baby food (if necessary)

Breastfeeding with a great view of the woods. [JEN AIST]

If you are a breastfeeding mom who uses a pump, there's a double pumping kit that can be used as a double hand pump. As long as you are moving the piston back and forth sixty times each minute, you are doing what the electric pump does. Be sure to boil the pump parts each night for five minutes.

If your baby drinks formula, you have a few options. You can bring out "ready-to-feed" formula so you don't need to add water at all. You can bring enough water from home to mix instant formula for the whole trip. Or you can treat water on the trail for mixing formula. In any case, be sure you boil the bottles and nipples each night at camp or bring new ones for each day.

If your baby is eating pureed baby foods, you'll need to put a little more thought into meal planning. For a day trip, bringing jarred baby food is fine, but you won't want to bring that many containers on an extended base-camp or backpacking adventure. For these trips, plan meals that can easily be smashed with a fork to make it the right consistency for your baby. A hand baby-food grinder works too.

Pausing for some baby food is easy, even on a day hike. [JEN AIST]

SUN

"The sun does not shine for a few trees and flowers, but for the wide world's joy."

—Henry Ward Beecher, *Life Thoughts*

*e*veryone loves a sunny day, and with some simple precautions, you and your children can enjoy it safely. Start by teaching your children safe sun habits when they're babies. More than 80 percent of solar damage to our skin occurs in the first eighteen years of life, and 90 percent of all skin cancer is caused by the sun. One bad sunburn as a child can double the chance of developing skin cancer later in life. Damage from the sun can and does occur even on cloudy days. So routine sun protection needs to be practiced every day.

HOW TO BE SUN SMART

The National Weather Service, along with the Environmental Protection Agency (EPA), has developed a system to predict ultraviolet (UV) radiation across the United States, because the amount varies widely across the country. This UV Index Forecast is available online and is frequently printed in the weather forecast section of local newspapers.

The EPA and dermatologists advise limiting exposure to direct sunlight between the hours of 10:00 AM and 4:00 PM, when the UV radiation is at its highest. Remember that snow, water, and sand reflect a significant amount of harmful rays, increasing the likelihood of sunburns.

The Cancer Council Victoria (Australia) promotes practicing the Five S's:
1. Slip on some protective clothing.
2. Slap on a hat.
3. Seek shade.
4. Slop on SPF 30 or higher sunscreen.
5. Slide on some sunglasses.

CLOTHING AS SUN ARMOR

The textile industry has created some fabulous materials to block the sun's harmful rays, and it uses an ultraviolet protection factor (UPF) rating system to designate a fabric's ability to filter UV rays. The highest allowable UPF rating is 50 plus. Most cotton T-shirts have a UPF rating of about 7 or 8, which means that 50 percent of harmful UV rays can still penetrate to the skin. Up to 50 percent more UV rays can penetrate the skin if that cotton T-shirt is wet from perspiration or water. Although it is more expensive than cotton, UPF clothing has a long life and provides great protection. It comes in many sizes and styles, including items for infants and toddlers. Invest in some of this protective clothing.

Hats are a powerful weapon in your arsenal of protective gear. Start getting your baby used to wearing a hat as early as possible. A wide-brimmed hat or one with a bandanna-like scarf in the back, called a legionnaire hat, offers excellent protection for the neck and ears. Many hat companies are using fabric with UPF now as well. When choosing a hat, look for one that does these things:

- Shades the face, neck, and ears
- Has close-weave fabric
- Is easy to keep on (consider windy adventures such as boat trips)
- Allows airflow to keep the head cool

WILD FACT
Windburn

There is no such thing as wind*burn*. The wind may dry your skin but cannot burn it.

- Crumples well when the baby wearing it is lying down (a legionnaire-style hat is great for this)

If the hat isn't comfortable, the child won't wear it. And if the child isn't wearing it, it won't protect him or her.

TAKING THE SHADE WITH YOU

You can buy a sun shade for most external-frame baby backpacks. Do it. Not only does it provide needed shade, it also protects the baby from weather and passing branches on the trail. Numerous sun shades are also available for strollers and baby joggers; they attach to the stroller top and come down over the front of the stroller.

Umbrellas offer easy, on-the-spot shade. Use them for sun, bug, and rain protection. Don't worry that you'll have to cart a full-sized umbrella on the

A lightweight tarp provides instant shade for this napping baby. [JEN AIST]

trail—ultralight models are available for backpacking. Black flies and gnats are attracted to dark colors, so a black underside has the added advantage of drawing bugs up and away from you and baby.

Tarps can be set up anywhere to provide instant shade. In the backcountry, lightweight tarps can be used for sun shades, rain protection, or ground cloths. If trees aren't available to tie off to, use your trekking poles instead.

TIPS & TRICKS

While many people may not have wide-brimmed sunhats on hand, chances are, most have old baseball caps lying around. Although baseball caps alone do not provide enough shade to the cheeks, ears, or neck, you can put a bandanna under a baseball cap to add protection.

SUNSCREEN BASICS

It may be invisible once you've rubbed it onto your little one, but sunscreen is an important barrier to the sun. No sunscreen provides 100 percent protection from UV radiation.

Many pediatricians advise not using sunscreen on infants younger than six months. Call your baby's doctor to find out his or her recommendation.

Most pediatricians agree that you should avoid sunscreens containing the compound known as PABA (para-aminobenzoic acid) due to possible allergic reaction.

Be aware that babies may react with a rash to sunscreens. When trying out a new

Legionnaire-style hats shield the neck and ears well. [TOM TWIGG]

brand, apply it on a small part of your baby's body first. If you notice anything unusual, stop using the product and contact your baby's doctor. Choosing products without fragrances or dyes will help avoid allergic reactions.

Marcia had been living in Hawaii for a year when she booked a whale-watching tour. She had used many different brands of sunscreen on her eight-month-old baby. As a rule, since her baby had many allergies, she always tested each brand on his foot or leg to check for a reaction. He had never had a negative reaction to any of the sunscreens she had used. On the morning of the whale-watching tour, they were minutes from boarding the boat when Marcia realized she had forgotten the sunscreen. She ran into a local shop and grabbed the only brand they had—one she had never used before. Confident that he wouldn't react to this sunscreen, she slopped it all over his body. Within twenty minutes her baby had broken out in hives all over his face and body. The swelling was so bad they were worried about his ability to breathe. They had to cancel their boat tour and instead spent the morning in the emergency room.

How Sunscreens Work

Basically there are two types of sunscreens: physical and chemical.

Physical sunscreens reflect or scatter both UVA and UVB rays before they have a chance to penetrate your skin. These sunscreens contain titanium dioxide and/or zinc oxide and are generally longer lasting and gentler to the skin than chemical sunscreens.

Chemical sunscreens absorb UV rays before they can cause any damage. These products contain ingredients such as avobenzone (Parsol 1789), oxybenzone, or mexoryl. While effective, chemical sunscreens break down easily and need to be reapplied even more frequently.

SPF Ratings

Regardless of the type of sunscreen you choose, you need to consider its sun protection factor (SPF), a rating for the amount of UVB protection it provides. (There is no rating system for UVA protection.) You want to use sunscreen with at least SPF 15.

The higher the SPF rating, the more protection. However, this does not mean that you can stay out in the sun longer with a higher SPF sunscreen on. In fact, SPF has nothing to do with how much time you can spend in the sun. SPF 15 filters out around 93 percent

ESSENTIAL GEAR CHECK
Sun Protection
- protective clothing, sunhat
- portable shade (optional)
- sunscreen
- sunglasses

of UVB rays, while SPF 30 filters out 97 percent. Because sunscreen effectiveness decreases over time, a couple of hours after application the difference in SPF between these two sunscreens is minimal.

Countdown: Important Numbers to Remember

3: Discard any bottles of sunscreen older than three years. The product is no longer stable or effective after this point.

2: Sunscreens need to be reapplied every two hours throughout the day, no matter what the directions say on the bottle. No sunscreen lasts all day. Always apply sunscreen liberally thirty minutes before you go outside.

1: For an adult, the recommendation is to apply one ounce, or about half a shot glass, of sunscreen for each application. You can scale that down for kids. I like to put sunscreen on baby's head, too—even if he's wearing a hat. Chances are pretty good he'll rip the hat off at some point, and most babies don't have enough hair to provide any protection to the scalp.

0: Even if there's no visible sunshine, practice sun protection habits. UV radiation has no trouble penetrating cloud cover.

EYE PROTECTION

With all this talk about skin, let us not forget our eyes. Ultraviolet radiation can also damage your eyes, causing cataracts, macular degeneration, or *pingue culae* (raised lesions on the white part of your eye). While more expensive sunglasses don't necessarily mean better protection, they often offer some nice features that justify the price tag:

- Straps to help them stay on heads
- Quality joints that don't break easily
- Quality lenses that resist scratches
- 100 percent UV protection

Likewise, the color or darkness of a lens does not indicate the level of UV protection. You have to read the labels carefully.

Get babies used to wearing sunglasses when they are younger than three months old so they'll be less likely to pull them off when they're a bit more coordinated.

HEAT-RELATED ILLNESSES

In hot environments, be very careful about overheating. Children, especially babies, are very susceptible to heat illnesses. To avoid them, keep baby cool and well hydrated.

Several factors influence people's ability to cool themselves. In highly humid environments, the body's natural cooling method of sweating doesn't work. It's like sweating underwater: the high moisture content in the air matches the sweat on your body, and evaporation no longer works. It's evaporation, not sweating itself, that cools the body. Babies sweat, too, but aren't as efficient at cooling themselves as adults are. Plus babies don't have as much surface area from which to sweat and cool off.

To make matters worse, all that sweating dehydrates the body very quickly. You sweat about half to one liter of fluid for every hour that you walk in the heat and two liters per hour when you hike in the direct sun. The best indicator of adequate hydration is the volume and color of urine. It should be copious and clear.

Wraparound sunglasses stay put on baby heads. [KAROLINE SCHNELL]

	HEAT EXHAUSTION	HEAT STROKE
Definition	When the body has had an excessive loss of the water and salt contained in sweat. If untreated, heat exhaustion will progress to heat stroke.	When the body is no longer able to regulate its temperature. As the body temperature rises, the sweating mechanism shuts down and the body can no longer cool itself.
Warning signs	Heavy sweating Paleness Muscle cramps Tiredness Weakness Dizziness Headache Nausea or vomiting Fainting	Extremely high body temperature (103 degrees F or higher, orally) Red, hot, dry skin (no sweating) Rapid, strong pulse Throbbing headache Dizziness Nausea Confusion Unconsciousness
What to do	Drink cool nonalcoholic beverages Rest Take a cool shower, bath, or sponge bath Wear lightweight clothing	Call for medical assistance while you begin doing the following: Get the victim into the shade. Cool the victim rapidly using any method available. For example, immerse the victim in water from a cool stream or creek, or use a spigot at a campground. Use soaked bandannas to sponge cool water over the victim. Monitor body temperature and continue cooling efforts until the body temperature drops to 101–102 degrees F. Do *not* give the victim fluids to drink.
Seek medical attention immediately:	If symptoms are severe If the victim has heart problems If the victim has high blood pressure	If the victim begins to twitch uncontrollably. Keep the victim from injuring him- or herself, but do *not* place any object in the mouth and do *not* give fluids. If the victim is vomiting, make sure the airway remains open by turning the victim on his or her side.

Sources: *National Park Service, Centers for Disease Control and Prevention*

Staying Hydrated

Don't wait until your baby is thirsty to start feeding him or her fluids. Once your baby is really thirsty, he or she is already dehydrated. If you notice your baby's diapers are wet less frequently or darker in color, your baby is already dehydrated.

To keep your baby hydrated, increase the amount of fluids to your babe. If you are nursing, offer the breast more often. You may find that your baby needs to nurse more frequently. Exclusively breastfed babies do not need any additional water; breast milk has all the water your baby needs. However, breastfeeding moms may need some extra water to maintain their hydration. Formula-fed babies more than three months old may benefit from an occasional bottle of water.

Your drink of choice for babies, toddlers, and preschoolers is always water. Don't use sweetened drink mixes. Sweet, sugary drinks actually make children lose more body fluids. Always bring extra water with you or a water filter to get more water along the trail.

A sun shade added to this child carrier offers extra protection to the baby. [JEN AIST]

Preventing Heat-related Illness

As always, your best bet is prevention. Start hydrating your baby at least twenty-four hours before your hike. Limit your activities around peak sun hours; plan to spend these hot hours somewhere in the shade lying low. Just follow the example of the critters: you usually don't see a lot of animals running around in the heat of the day. Feed your children a quick salty snack like pretzels every time you stop to take a drink of water, to give their bodies much-needed salts and energy.

Korin had a difficult time getting her toddler to take naps during the heat of the day when they went on camping trips in the tropical climate of Darwin, Australia. There are few shade trees in Darwin, and tents can become ovens in the midday sun. Korin's solution was to take a drive in the air-conditioned car during the hottest parts of the day. This gave everyone a break from the sun and the heat and allowed their toddler a comfortable nap.

If you recognize the early signs of heat illness, you and your children can avoid heat exhaustion and heat stroke altogether. The preceding table defines the signs and symptoms of both heat exhaustion and heat stroke. Pay attention to their symptoms so you can recognize them if necessary.

Living in Alaska where it's winter half of the year, I have a special appreciation for hot, sunny days. But I've also lived in the Central Valley of California, where average summer temperatures are more than 100 degrees F by 8:00 AM, so I know how hard on the body a lot of heat can be. With some common sense and "sun smarts," we can all safely enjoy the heat of summer.

BUGS

"Mama, why did God have to make bugs anyway?"
—Ian, age four, 2:00 AM on the Denali Highway
when we ran out of antihistamine

9've read scores of books about camping with young children, but none of them devote more than a paragraph or two to the subject of tiny insects biting you or your child. My conclusion? The authors never camped with mosquitoes in the Alaska backcountry or the Florida Everglades.

Mosquitoes are not your only enemy, though. Hornets, yellow jackets, ticks, blackflies, no-see-ums, gnats, and spiders all want a piece of your child's soft flesh. Itchy skin is not fun for anyone, not to mention the potential diseases that bugs can transmit. Plan A is to avoid bites and stings in the first place. Then have a Plan B for dealing with an uncomfortable kid when Plan A doesn't work.

Adult-sized bug suits work just fine on little kids. [JEN AIST]

AVOIDING BITES AND STINGS

There are many simple and effective techniques to avoid flying bugs like mosquitoes, gnats, blackflies, and no-see-ums. For prevention tips for other types of insects, see "Bugs to Watch Out For."

Bug Netting

I love bug netting. You can't have too much of it. It's cheap, easy to use, and totally chemical-free. Never go out camping—or even day hiking—without netting. Several companies make bug suits sized for the whole family.

Stroller netting can be placed over anything. I've wrapped it over strollers, camp chairs, kayak cockpits, and more. I like to use the double stroller size, which is big enough to wrap around whatever the kids happen to be sitting in at the time. At home, I even use the netting to cover the infant swing when I bring it outside on the deck. If the net is too big, you can cinch it up, but it won't work at all if it is too small.

Jill travels frequently in small planes to remote areas in Alaska's bush, places that are inundated with mosquitoes and no-see-ums. When she is carrying her daughter in a front carrier, Jill takes an extra-large-sized netting and puts it over both of them. This way they are both well protected.

Work on getting crawling-age babies and toddlers used to wearing a wide-brimmed hat or a baseball hat at as young an age as possible so you can drape a head net over the hat. Otherwise, head nets without hats just hang on kids' faces and can really annoy

Some netting and a camp chair make for a perfect nap spot. [JEN AIST]

them. Simple head nets are cheap, are sold everywhere, and go far in protecting you and your kids from bug bites.

Tent Care

Make sure your tent, including its bug screens, is in good shape to keep you free from bugs at night. Bring duct tape with you for temporarily patching holes; it can be a real lifesaver. I've known more than one family who forgot the dog in the tent, and dogs are great for ripping big holes in tent screens when they want out.

According to the Centers for Disease Control and Prevention, the mosquitoes that are the most important vectors for (carriers of) the West Nile virus are most active from dusk to dawn. In other words, they are most active at night when you are sleeping. Keep your tent in good shape to keep mosquitoes out.

Extra-large bug netting protects both mom and baby. [JILL BOYD]

Clothing Tricks

Light-colored clothing deters bugs a bit, while dark-colored clothing attracts bugs. Nylon material is great for the backcountry. It is lightweight and durable, dries quickly, and is tough for insects to bite through. You can even find nylon pants and suits for young children. They aren't cheap, but they will last a long time.

Just as with sun protection, long-sleeved shirts and long pants go far in protecting your skin from bugs. If it is hot out, clothing that offers good protection will be preferable to bug bites as long as the clothing is lightweight. A wet bandanna wrapped around the neck can help provide additional protection for your little one while also providing some heat relief—two-for-one!

Insect Repellents

If only there were a magic elixir that would deter all biting and stinging insects without harming us. However, what we have available is a dozen or more mixes, either herbal or chemical, that help to varying degrees. You'll probably have to purchase several before you find one your family likes. Always check with your pediatrician before using any chemicals on your baby or young child.

Many companies make natural repellents, but keep in mind that "natural" does not automatically imply "safe." A large number of people are sensitive to plant oils. All of the herbal repellents need to be reapplied frequently, usually every couple of hours. The exception is lemon eucalyptus, which should not be applied more than twice daily. Always read the label for any and all warnings.

Of the chemical repellents, there are basically two kinds on the market:

Picaridin (2-2-hydroxyethyl-1-piperidinecarboxylic acid 1-methylpropyl ester) has been commercially available for only a few years. It is supposed to be as effective as DEET against biting flies, mosquitoes, chiggers, and ticks without the smell. It is generally considered to be a more "gentle" chemical to the skin, with a lower toxicity rating.

DEET (di-ethyl toluamide) is an oily colorless liquid that is effective against flying insects and ticks. It comes in varying strengths, ranging from 4 percent to 100 percent. For years the recommendation was *no* DEET for children. Recently, however, the American Academy of Pediatrics has issued a statement that DEET concentrations of 10 percent to 30 percent are safe when used appropriately for children older than two months. They recommend using the lowest effective concentration of DEET and never using a product that combines DEET with a sunscreen. This doesn't mean you can't use sunscreen and DEET; just avoid products that have the two mixed into one formula.

Other precautions for the use of DEET include these:

- Do not apply over open wounds, abrasions, or irritated skin.
- Do not apply to hands or near eyes or mouth of young children.
- Do not use under clothing.
- Avoid prolonged or excessive use. Do not apply DEET more than once a day.
- Apply sparingly.
- Wash treated skin with soap and water.
- Wash treated clothing before wearing it again.
- Do not spray in an enclosed area.

FINDING RELIEF FROM ITCHES AND STINGS

I guarantee that your baby or child will get bug bites despite all of your efforts to avoid them. So never go on a hike or extended trip without anti-itch products with you. Consult your pediatrician about using over-the-counter 1 percent cortisone ointment to apply directly to bug bites or antihistamines to combat itching and inflammation from bug bites. Both can really help relieve the itch. Aveeno makes a good anti-itch cream, and there's always good old-fashioned calamine lotion. I'm a big fan of Hyland's Bug Bite Ointment; it comes in a stick similar to lip balm, so it fits easily in your pack. It has a very light scent, and my kids tell me it really helps to alleviate the itch. For other types of treatment for bug encounters, see the next section.

BUGS TO WATCH OUT FOR

Don't let bugs deter you from getting out into nature. Although some encounters are nearly unavoidable—mosquitoes, for instance, seem to be everywhere—most bugs aren't that common. And while it is necessary to be aware of the potential diseases bugs can carry, you are far less likely to fall ill from them than you are from touching germs on an office desk, your kitchen sink, or an escalator handle.

Mosquitoes

The United States is home to more than 200 species of mosquitoes, all of which have their own unique habitat. It is the female mosquito that bites us, to get blood to nourish her eggs. (Knowing this gives me only the slightest amount of sympathy for the bug before I slap it dead with my hand.)

ESSENTIAL GEAR CHECK
Bug Protection

- protective netting
- screened tent or shelter
- protective clothing, gaiters
- insect repellent
- anti-itch treatment, antihistamine

Mosquitoes are known to carry many diseases. The most common of these illnesses in the United States is West Nile virus. Documented cases have been reported as of 2008 in every state except Alaska, Hawaii, Maine, and North Carolina.

Bees and Wasps

No one likes to be stung by a bee or a wasp. It really hurts! And if you are like me, you will cry as much as your baby if she gets stung. Bug netting can help prevent stings from happening in the first place. Should one get through, the treatment is very straightforward: scrape the stinger off (only honeybees leave the stinger in your skin), wash with soap and water, and consider giving an antihistamine. (Talk to your pediatrician about antihistamine doses and uses.) Ice can help with the pain and swelling as well.

Ticks

Ticks like mild climates, especially those with tall grass, and they can be found in many parts of the world. There are many species of ticks, which, like spiders and scorpions, have eight legs. Many of the insect repellents that deter mosquitoes, such as 10 percent to 30 percent DEET, deter ticks as well. Here are other ways to protect your little ones when you are traveling through tick country:

- Tuck their pant legs into their socks, so the ticks can't reach skin.
- Wear gaiters, which strap to your boot and go up your lower leg, either halfway or all the way to the knee, for even more protection.
- Check your child's feet, ankles, and arms frequently to make sure he or she doesn't have an extra passenger. Disease transmission from ticks takes about four hours after the bite, so if you find the ticks early enough—either before they've lodged in the skin or soon after—you don't need to worry about disease.

There are numerous old wives' tales about how to properly remove a tick attached to your skin. Some say to twist it out clockwise; others, counterclockwise. Some say to hold a hot match to the tick's head or to cover the head with petroleum jelly. Don't do any of these! Not only do they not work, they may actually make matters worse by causing the tick to expel more saliva and pathogens into your skin, increasing your chances of becoming ill. Once you've noticed the tick, here's the only approved method of removing it and dealing with the afteraffects:

- Using tweezers, grasp the tick as close to the skin as you can.
- Pull upward slowly with steady, even pressure.
- Don't handle ticks with your bare hands.
- Place the tick in a resealable plastic bag. Once at home, label the bag with the date of the hike and where you were hiking and place it in your freezer.

In the event that anyone does get ill, having the tick will help your doctor determine what kind of tick it was and exactly which disease you might have. Ticks carry many diseases, including Lyme disease. The incubation period for most tick-borne diseases is five to ten days. Be on the lookout for symptoms such as fever, headache, muscle ache, and the telltale bull's-eye rash around the bite during this time period. If you observe any of them, call your doctor.

Chiggers

Chiggers, also known as harvest mites or red bugs, are extremely small bugs that cannot be seen without a magnifying glass. They have six legs and no wings, and their bite causes severe itching. Chiggers are mainly found in the southern United States, in tall grass and berry patches.

Insect repellents, long pants, and long-sleeved shirts all offer nice protection. If your children or you have been playing in chigger country, it is wise to rinse off at the end of the day. Chiggers are easily wiped away with your hand or with water.

While chiggers carry no disease, their bites can become infected, and therefore bites should be kept clean. Chigger bites will appear as a rash focused around waistlines and armpits; the rash looks a lot like chicken pox, but chicken pox is associated with a fever a few days prior to breaking out in a rash that is frequently first seen at the base of the neck. No treatment is needed for the chigger rash other than relief from the itch.

Spiders

Most folks don't like spiders. The truth is that most spiders are friendly and beneficial to ecosystems. At least that's what Charlotte taught us all in *Charlotte's Web*. They actually do a great job at bug control. As is the case with most creepy crawlers, spiders like to hang out in dark, sheltered areas. They don't seek out humans. We move into their space, and they respond defensively.

Teach children to look before sticking their hands into logs, holes, and old wood piles. It can also be a good idea to shake out your sleeping bag, clothes, and shoes before getting into them. Most spider bites cause nothing more than redness, swelling, itching, and maybe a little soreness, which can all be treated as with any other insect bite. But there are a couple of poisonous spiders to be aware of in the United States: the black widow and the brown recluse.

The black widow can be identified by a shiny black body with a reddish

WILD FACT
Spider Webs

If a spider wanted to spin a single strand around the world, it would take forty-one years and eight months, given a spin speed of 6 feet per minute. The entire strand would weigh less than a pound.

hourglass shape on her underside. Black widows are about a half inch long. Only the female black widow spider is dangerous to humans, but despite her infamous Hollywood reputation, very few people die from her bite. According to the California Poison Action Line, no one has died in the past ten years from a black widow bite. In fact, the spider does not always inject venom at all. If you or your child does get bitten by a black widow, wash the wound thoroughly with soap and water. If any symptoms such as severe muscle pain or cramps develop in the first couple hours after the bite, head to the hospital. Black widow spider antivenin is available though seldom necessary.

The brown recluse can be differentiated from the many other species of brown spiders by its markings—or, rather, the lack thereof: the brown recluse has *no* markings on the tail end of its body. If you see any markings at all, it is just a regular brown spider. Only the brown recluse is dangerous. A bite from one of these eight-legged critters is distinguished by a blister with a red ring around it and a white ring around the red ring, giving it a bull's-eye appearance. Treatment consists of simply washing the wound with soap and water and applying a topical antibiotic ointment. Watch for fever, chills, generalized rash, and weakness. Get to a doctor if symptoms worsen.

Scorpions

Scorpions are small, and their tan color makes them difficult to see in the desert environments where they are common. Stings do occur, but you can avoid stings by teaching your children to shake out their boots and clothing before dressing, to wear shoes (even in camp), and to shake out their bedding before climbing into it. While scorpion stings are painful, they rarely cause serious health problems. The elderly and very young children are most susceptible to their venom. If stung, apply cool compresses to the sting site (for pain relief) and monitor the victim. It is rare for an evacuation to be necessary.

DIRT

"What I like about camping is you can get really dirty. Either you're all by yourself, so no one else sees you, or everyone you're with is just as dirty as you are, so nobody cares."

—anonymous former Boy Scout

Part of the joy of playing in the woods is getting dirty. Research shows that spontaneous, unstructured play in the dirt is not only fun, it is beneficial and even essential to proper growth and development of young children. So let them get dirty! Some people spend significant amounts of money to take mud baths at fancy spas—that's how good it feels to have all that silky mud oozing all over you.

My family spent one memorable afternoon on the shores of the McClaren River near the Amphitheater Mountains in interior Alaska. The river feeds directly from the McClaren Glacier, which gives the river a fantastic glacial green color and churns up lots of glacial silt—fabulous mud to play in! It is so soft that you can't help but dig your hands into it. It was a hot, sunny day and the mud puddles on the side of the river were calling our names. It wasn't long till all six of us—actually eight, if you include the dogs—were covered head to toe in mud! We rolled in it, painted our arms with it, and simply sat in it. We didn't have any toys with us. We just used sticks and leaves and materials from nature to augment our play. And as an added bonus, the mud kept the mosquitoes at bay. We had a marvelously muddy afternoon.

Like so many good things, a muddy adventure like this has to come to a close before you can get in your sleeping bags. So let's talk about how to get clean in the woods.

HAND WASHING

Children should be encouraged to get dirty and make mud pies and check out big banana slugs. But kids and adults alike should wash their hands before and after eating, whether it's snacktime or mealtime. Using running water and soap is the best way to wash hands, and hand washing is the single most effective defense against illness.

If you are car camping, you can set up a five-gallon water jug with a spigot on a picnic table, with a wastewater collection container underneath it. Turn the flow on a trickle, lather up with some liquid soap, and wash away.

If you are camping in the backcountry, you can set up a similar but smaller system, using a collapsible water jug set on a log or rock. Be sure to use biodegradable soap, and dispose of the water at least 200 feet from natural water sources.

For a quick washup on the trail, waterless hand sanitizers are quite effective in killing bacteria and viruses on the skin. Bottled sanitizer is easy to pack, and due to its primary ingredient of alcohol, it won't freeze!

TOILETING

Even on short day hikes, you and your children might have to deal with waste disposal, and that will involve different techniques, depending on their age.

Diapering

Changing diapers on the trail isn't a big deal. Normally I recommend using wipes without alcohol or fragrances to protect tender baby skin. However, for camping I use wipes with alcohol for disinfectant. Here are some helpful diapering guidelines:

1. Put together a diaper sack with all your supplies in one place. This will include the same supplies you

Getting really muddy is marvelously fun.
[HEIDI BARKER]

typically check for in your diaper bag: diapers, wipes, cream, hand sanitizer, plastic baggies for soiled diapers, a changing pad (this is not strictly necessary but nice). Have this sack at the ready. You don't want to have to dig through your whole pack to get to the diaper sack.

2. Change your baby frequently to avoid diaper rash. Bathing daily on multiday trips isn't always possible, so make sure you wipe well. Sand, shale, and dirt stuck in the diaper can really irritate infant skin. Take the time to pick off all the irritants.

3. Whenever possible, dump any solid material into an outhouse or bury it per the Leave No Trace guidelines in your area: in a cat hole dug 6 to 8 inches deep and at least 200 feet from water, camp, or trails (guidelines for different ecosystems such as desert, tundra, sea coast, and more are available from the Leave No Trace website—see Resources).

4. What can't get dumped gets wrapped up in a diaper and tossed in a resealable plastic bag for disposal back at the trailhead, campground, or home. Consider putting this plastic bag in a nylon stuff sack to avoid having the plastic bag break. All dirty diapers, used wipes, and used toilet paper get packed out. Hopefully

Portable potty seats are great for car camping. [JEN AIST]

it doesn't need to be said that you should tie the dirty diaper bag onto the *outside* of your pack.

Hauling a week's worth of dirty diapers out of the backcountry can be quite cumbersome. I know families who use cloth diapers when they camp so they don't have to carry out any dirties. To wash them, pack a small plastic bin or a collapsible sink, and use biodegradable soap. Be sure to dispose of the wastewater as in step 3 above. Regular cloth diapers dry faster than the prefolds. Jo, a mom of seven, used to pin the drying diapers to the packs of her children while they were hiking to speed up the drying process. If you're anticipating lots of rain, which will make it harder to get the diapers dry, you may be better off using disposables.

Potty Training

Potty training isn't the easiest time to take toddlers out camping. Newly potty-trained kids tend to have more potty accidents when they are distracted, and camping is one big distraction. If you're on an adventure during this phase, be sure you remind your child to potty often on the trail.

If you're lucky, your child will be OK squatting in the woods with the usual backcountry methods described in steps 3 and 4 under "Diapering." Be sure to have children wash their hands afterward, even if it's just with hand sanitizer.

For the child who is particular about his or her potty, we have other creative solutions. I know parents who carry a potty seat and prop it on branches over a cat hole to make an outdoor seat "more like home." One toddler on a rafting trip wanted her seat off the ground. The solution: her parents cut a hole in the bottom of a five-gallon plastic bucket, then they fitted a toddler-sized potty seat on top of it. Voila! Comfort potty in the wilderness!

The summer my twins potty trained, we did a lot of car and base camping. We brought the little potty chair with us. During the night, I put it just outside the tent so we wouldn't have to go as far as to the outhouse in the middle of the night. (Because the potty chair is covered, you don't need to worry about insects as you do with urinating on the ground.)

Also, I was really worried my twins might have an accident in their sleeping bags, so I stopped giving them liquids an hour or so before bed, then had them potty a couple of times before settling in for the night.

Large Backcountry Groups

If you are camping outside of an established campground with a large group (which could be as few as four to six people), there are some special considerations when it comes to toileting.

Large-group backpacking trips are best on established trail systems equipped with outhouses or in areas where Leave No Trace waste disposal methods are acceptable (see steps 3 and 4 in "Diapering").

For base camping, when you have been dropped off somewhere, or on river trips, often all waste needs to be packed out. Thanks to modern technology, this isn't as bad as it sounds. Several companies make portable toilets with odor-proof, biodegradable bags. The size and weight of these portable toilet systems are not feasible on a backpacking trip, but they are great for other types of trips.

At your base camp, set up the bathroom at least 200 feet from your sleeping and cooking areas and any water sources. Station a roll of toilet paper and some waterless hand sanitizer in a waterproof container or resealable plastic bag on the way to the bathroom or next to the potty. To increase the efficiency of the potty's composting system, store dirty toilet paper in a separate resealable plastic bag. For privacy, you can set up a small tent or tarp around the potty. It is often easier just to set up a signaling system to let others know the bathroom is occupied. Kimmer, a longtime kayaking guide,

Brushing teeth in the woods involves just a little more forethought than doing it at home. [JEN AIST]

recommends leaving the toilet paper bag on the way to the potty: when you are going to use the bathroom, if the bag isn't there, the potty is occupied; if the bag is there, the potty is available. When you're done, wash your hands and put the bag back in its place for the next user.

At the conclusion of your trip, secure the portable potty bag well. This is one bag you don't want to leak. Dispose of the waste properly according to the directions of the potty system manufacturer; many potty bags can be disposed of in pit toilets.

DENTAL HYGIENE

Camping is no time to let your babes skimp on dental hygiene. Put all toothbrushes and toothpaste in one resealable plastic bag and store it with your food, because toothpaste carries a food scent for animals. If you are backpacking, store these items in a bear box or hang them to avoid attracting wildlife. If you are car camping, store them in either the car or a food cache, as each campground dictates.

Make sure you have your children spit at least 200 feet from water sources, your camp, or trails, and dilute and disperse toothpaste spit. If you are in an area with an approved fire ring, it is generally OK to spit in it, but ask the campground host first. Always check with local authorities about proper disposal of all wastewater—which includes spit from teeth-brushing—for that particular environment.

BATHING

Bathing can be as convenient as getting in the heated shower of your RV or the campground showers or as inaccessible

A plastic bin makes for a perfect bathtub in the pop-up trailer. [ANNE FONTANA]

as not being able to shower at all for a few days or more. If you are someone who has to bathe daily, pick your destination carefully. Not all campgrounds have showers.

Car Camping

While car camping, bathing babies and small children is a simple matter of bringing along a big plastic bin and filling it with warm soapy water (use small amounts of biodegradable soap). If the campground doesn't have warm water on tap, heat some on your camp stove. It doesn't take as long as you would think, because a baby doesn't need that much water to bathe in. Follow the campground guidelines for disposal of soapy water.

You can administer a pretty thorough sponge bath with this same bucket method.

- biodegradable soap
- washtub (optional)
- hand sanitizer, towelettes (optional)
- diapers, wipes, diaper cream (if necessary)
- toilet paper
- portable potty (optional)
- toothbrushes, toothpaste, dental floss
- washcloth or bandanna, camp towel
- cord for clothesline (clothespins optional)
- hair brush, comb

Don't worry too much if little fingers pick up dirt and leaves along with berries. [RAYNA SWANSON]

For a quick washup after meals or before naps, heat up some water on the camp stove and wash everyone's hands and faces. Bandannas make great washcloths! Bring along some clothesline, such as parachute cord, and some clothespins to hang out wet items to dry. It feels great to get a bit of grime, sunscreen, and bug dope off of you before jumping in the sleeping bag.

For kids with enough hair to tie up, put it in nice, tight braids or ponytails to keep it from getting out of control. After a five-day raft trip, my daughter's braids still remained, despite how much wind and silt they withstood. The braids really saved her from some major tangles. When I helped her wash her hair at home, glacial silt just streamed out into the shower.

If the climate is warm and sunny, sun showers can be quite the luxury. Sun showers are plastic bags that hold a gallon or so of water; hang it from a tree and leave out all day to warm up. When the water is just the right temperature, turn on the nozzle; gravity controls the flow of water. You can even get little stand-up privacy tents or hang up a tarp to provide privacy while showering. It's important to clean young skin of all the day's sunscreen and bug dope, and a shower is a great way to do this.

In the Backcountry

You can give your little one a very effective sponge bath in the backcountry; you just need to be more conservative with the water. Heat up water on your stove and use a pack towel or bandanna to scrub down. Some families simply use diaper wipes at the end of the day for a quick cleanup; just remember to pack out your trash.

You can also wash your children's hair on backpacking trips. Bring along a compact pack towel and some biodegradable shampoo. Heat up water on the camp stove and find a spot well away from camp and any water sources. Have your child bend down on her knees and flip her hair over her head, then pour the water on, lather up, and rinse.

SLEEP

"O bed! O bed! Delicious bed! That heaven upon earth to the weary head."

—Thomas Hood, *Miss Kilmanseg—Her Dream*

Sleeping while on the trail, whether napping during day hikes or spending the night camping in a tent or shelter, is not the same as sleeping at home. The challenges with your children's sleep on the trail are these:

- Creating a safe sleeping space
- Keeping the bugs off
- Keeping your child warm
- Helping your child get a good rest

NAPS

Generally, young babies sleep during most of a hike. Some families start hiking around naptime and base the length of the hike on the amount of time their baby will sleep.

Toddlers will be awake more of the time, but they may need to take a nap along the trail even during a day hike. Always allow enough time for lots of breaks and naps. If you aren't carrying them in a child carrier or hauling them in a baby jogger or trailer, you'll need to arrange a sleep space on the trail. This can be as simple as laying a coat, an emptied backpack, or blankets out for them to lie on. Consider bringing along a packable hammock and enjoy napping with your child in it. Although you might be tempted at times to skip the nap and just power on to your destination, don't. Over-tired kids are cranky kids. And cranky, tired kids are not fun to hang out with. They also tend to be more accident-prone.

SETTING UP CAMP

No one cherishes their sleep more than parents of young children, and after a long day of hiking and playing with your kids, your sleeping bag will call to you louder than an oasis in a desert. But first you need to set up camp. Always allow enough time to set up your camp before nightfall. You are on kid time now.

Tent Considerations

Choosing your campsite is easy when you're car camping, right? However, campgrounds can be noisy places at night, and chances are, your child will go to bed before the quiet hours begin. If your child is sensitive to sound, choose a campsite on the outer loops to substantially minimize the amount of noise. Pick a site away from spots with increased traffic. Some parents say the hum of RV generators actually acts as white noise. Others bring small radios or white noise machines to play during sleep time to buffer the outside noise.

When you're in the backcountry, make sure your campsite is well situated to leave no trace: 200 feet from the trail and water sources. In bear country, separate your tent site from your cooking and eating area by 100 feet; it's also a good idea to secure your food another 100 feet away from both, in a triangular arrangement with your cooking area downwind from your tent site.

Either in a campground or the backcountry, a restful night's sleep begins with a good tent site. Make sure it is level and not in a low spot. Look all around for any possible drainages heading toward your tent.

We were car camping once when evening thundershowers flooded our campsite. Our tent, which was nice and level, was located exactly where all the water in the whole campground seemed to pool. This happened after all the kids were in their pajamas, in their sleeping bags, and ready for bed. We had to evacuate the tent and relocate. Imagine if that happened after everyone was asleep at 2:00 AM! Had we planned a bit better, we could have stayed nice and dry in our tent and watched the storm pass.

Organize your tent and keep it that way. An organized tent helps you to find things quickly when you need them during the night.

Take extra care to keep the screen on your tent door closed all the time to keep bugs out, so you're not swatting at them all night.

Cabin Considerations

If you are cabin camping, make sure you know ahead of time how the bunks are arranged. Most public-use cabins or fire lookouts have pictures or descriptions of the interior available at the public lands office or other reservation location. With infants and toddlers, a full-size (double) bottom bunk is preferable. This way, you can sleep next to your little one and protect him or her from falling off the bunk. Single-wide bunks are pretty tight for two. If single bunks or top bunks are the only option, consider sleeping on the floor instead; most top bunks have little or no railing to keep young ones in place.

Also, unless you keep the woodstove going all night, cabins are generally colder than tents, because they're a larger area to heat. Dress accordingly.

Trailer and RV Considerations

Here are some easy ways to create safe sleep spaces while camping in a trailer or camper:

- Rail off motorhome or tent trailer beds with a travel bed rail that wedges under the mattress and extends upward around 10 inches.
- Use tension-mounted child gates to create a secure space at the edge of the bed.

A portable playpen and a travel bed rail can turn an RV couch into a child-safe sleep space.
[MICHELLE WAGNER]

- With younger infants, place a portable playpen right in the camper. Be sure to get the bug netting that fits the playpen so you can use it outside for naps during the day.
- If you can't create any kind of safety rail, make a "nest" on the floor of the camper with blankets or sleep pads. Parents can also sleep with their babies on their mattress.

SLEEP PADS, SLEEPING BAGS, AND OTHER OPTIONS

Sleep pads add an important layer of insulation and a barrier to wet ground, so be sure each sleeper has one, especially in cold, wet, or snowy conditions. Closed-cell foam pads or combination air-foam pads are the best. Straight air mattresses, such as the kind you might use in a guest room in your house, provide very limited warmth and tend to leak. They also pose a risk for babies, who might roll into their dips and potentially block their airways. Always be aware of any soft item that could block your baby's airway. Remember, oxygen is a beautiful thing!

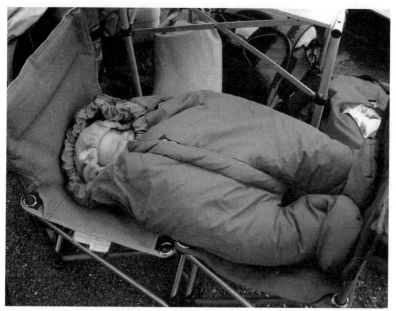

Baby bags, small sleeping bags for babies, are great for naps or overnights. [JEN AIST]

You have several options for your baby's bedding:

Poly-filled nylon baby-sized sleeping bags. These are not made anymore because they are not safe to use in car seats, but you can find them in secondhand stores; they are perfect for camping. They go for about $5–$10 each.

Shelled snowsuits. A fleece snowsuit alone is not adequate to keep a baby warm on a cold night, but a snowsuit with a shell is. Bundled up in a snowsuit or baby bag, your baby can sleep next to you on his or her own sleep pad.

Bag doublers. Another option is to sleep with your baby. More companies than ever before are making bag doublers—a wedge-shaped piece of sleeping bag that enlarges the size of your mummy bag to easily accommodate you and a child or even two adults. Some of the larger doublers can be zipped closed by themselves to make a child-sized sleeping bag that would fit a child until about four years of age.

Sleep systems. If a bag doubler isn't large enough, sleep systems are available that zip two rectangular adult sleeping bags together to make one full-size (double)

Bag doublers convert your individual sleeping bag into a family sleeping bag. [JEN AIST]

sleeping bag. Your sleeping pads slip into a pocket on the bottom. Other bags are made double-wide to begin with. Several companies make these systems. The downside is that the whole top end of the bag is open. You lose the mummy effect around your neck, which means you lose some warmth. This is not a problem in warmer climates, but it can be a big concern in colder areas. Double-wide bags have enough room for two parents and a baby or a small child to sleep in.

Or you can pop your baby right in your single bag with you. This is certainly the warmest option for your baby. Many families report that their babies are so warm in their bags that they dress them in only a single layer of polypro. If your baby is used to sleeping in a crib with a lot of room to him- or herself, this is probably not the best option though. Be careful that your baby's head is not buried inside the bag. Your baby always needs to have clear access to air.

If you will be breastfeeding from your sleeping bag, you'll have to unzip the side during feeding, so wear an extra layer. I've known several moms who cut small slits in their polypro tops to turn their base layer into a nursing top. This is a great idea for staying warmer on chilly nights. When the baby is done nursing, just slide her head up next to yours, zip up your bag, and go back to sleep.

By age two, your child will need a bag of his or her own—some children at an even younger age. Most child-sized bags are designed for someone about 5 feet tall. This is obviously too long for most toddlers or preschoolers. To shorten the length of the bag, tie off the bottom with a piece of webbing. This will make the bag warmer for your child and eliminate the chance of your toddler getting lost in the bottom of the bag.

TIPS & TRICKS

When choosing a bag, keep in mind that you will likely get eight to twelve years of service out of it, so it will be a pretty good investment.

A 15- to 30-degree F bag is suitable for most environments. Warm climates can allow you to get away with a 40-degree F bag or even just a bag liner.

Make sure the bag has no cotton on it anywhere. Remember, cotton is cold when wet and takes forever to dry. Quite a few bags on the market have cotton liners, so read the labels closely. I would not recommend a down bag for a young child. Although warm and lightweight, down takes a long time to dry and loses its warmth when it gets wet—which sleeping bags frequently do, from damp conditions as well as from potty accidents in the night. Make your life a lot easier and get a poly-filled bag.

SLEEPWEAR

Staying warm and dry all night long is critical. Remember, even places where the day-time temperatures reach the triple digits, nighttime temps can hover around the freezing mark. Layering clothing works well for kids of any age.

For infants younger than one year old, start with a onesie (preferably of wool or synthetic fabric), wool socks that are not too tight around the ankle, and then add a polyester one-piece pajama suit. A warm cap will make a huge difference in keeping your baby warm. Make sure the hat has no strings that could shift and strangle the baby in the night. Additional layers will depend on where your baby sleeps—in his or her own baby bag or in a bag with you.

For toddlers, slipper (one-piece) pajamas are fine for boys, but girls have to take the whole thing off to potty, which can be really chilly. Consider two-piece pajamas for girls instead. Keep a warm hat for you and your child handy in case someone gets cold. Some parents sleep with an extra layer of baby or toddler clothes next to them. This way, if your child is chilled in the night, you can easily help them put on an additional layer already warmed by Mom or Dad.

SAFETY TIP

Never allow your child to eat in his or her sleeping bag. Any food scent will attract wildlife and put both your child and the animal at risk.

GETTING A GOOD NIGHT'S SLEEP WITH YOUR CHILDREN

If you know your child is very sensitive to changes in the sleep routine, tread lightly! Start with a trial night in the tent set up in your backyard. Experiment with different sleeping arrangements while you're in reach of your house.

Infants

If young babies sleep for most of the day's hike, this could mean that they will be awake most of the night. Some families plan shorter hikes for this very reason.

I've known many families who have cut their trips short and vowed never to go out again because of the sleep issue. Babies who are used to being in their own room in their own crib don't always adapt well to tent or cabin sleeping. If your baby doesn't do well sharing a sleeping space, you need to get a bit more creative at nighttime.

If there is room on a car-camping, base-camping, or paddling trip for a portable playpen, it can be a lifesaver. Try to not have the playpen right up against the wall of the tent so that heavy rain won't leak in. Be sure to bundle the baby up really well.

You might want to use a tent that comes with different "rooms" in it. Typically, these tents have a layer of nylon separating two compartments within the same tent. Set aside one for baby's sleeping area.

If your baby needs a totally dark sleep environment, consider bringing along some black nylon (available at most fabric stores) and attaching it to the ceiling inside your tent. It isn't a perfect system, but it does darken the tent somewhat. Light is a big concern for northern campers where the sun doesn't set until very late. Folks camping at more southerly latitudes could try this technique to keep the baby asleep later in the morning.

One mom I know brings along a small pup tent that she sets up inside their tent to put the baby in. This creates a separate sleep area that can be covered with a cloth to darken it. You could also use it outside the tent for naps.

While babies with sensitive sleep routines require more creativity, don't let that deter you from getting out. If the first night doesn't go well, review your options and try again. It will work eventually. I promise!

All worn out and ready for sleep snuggled in their own bags [JEN AIST]

Keep a dry diaper, wipes, hand sanitizer, and a plastic bag handy for infants who may need a midnight change. Having your headlamp handy will make this job much easier. Put all these diaper essentials in a small sack that's ready to go when needed.

Toddlers and Preschoolers

Toddlers and preschoolers tend to have more established sleep routines and therefore are a bit more adaptable to sleeping in camp. However, routine is still important. Find creative ways to duplicate the *actions* you use in your sleep routines at home.

For example, if your child loves to be rocked to sleep, try using a backpacking chair (a soft-sided folding canvas seat that supports your back while you're sitting on the ground). When you lean back in one of these, it becomes a perfect rocker. If your toddler loves to fall asleep hearing stories, bring along some books—or, better yet, make up some stories.

ESSENTIAL GEAR CHECK
Naps & Overnights

- pup tent or portable playpen with netting (optional)
- screened tent (multiroomed optional)
- travel bed rail or child gate (optional)
- sleep pads
- backpacking chair (optional)
- sleeping bags or bedding
- sleepwear
- headlamps

Consider creating some special routines that happen only when you camp. If you are camping somewhere where it gets dark early at night, start a shadow puppet show tradition before bed, or sing some favorite camp songs.

Be on the lookout for early signs that your child is getting tired. Don't push a tired child. Accidents happen with overtired kids, and there are plenty of hazards around camp.

When we camp, each child has a sleep sack for a clean pair of pajamas that have not been around any food, a favorite stuffed animal, a book, and a headlamp. We also allow each child to have one water bottle with a secure lid in the tent. If we are camping near water or in heavy rain, we pack the sleep sack in a dry bag; otherwise, we just use a stuff sack. Even a two-year-old can be taught to be responsible for his or her own sleep sack. Sleep sacks really help organize your tent and help your children to keep track of their gear.

Teach your children this: "Take care of your gear and your gear will take care of you."

Be sure your potty-trained child potties before bed. Midnight potty runs aren't much fun. If you do need to make that late-night potty run, have your shoes ready to grab by the tent door. Remember to move well away from the tent for pottying so the urine doesn't attract flies. If an outhouse or bathroom is available, use it.

Keep some anti-itch cream close by in case your little one gets to scratching in the middle of the night. And always keep your headlamp handy.

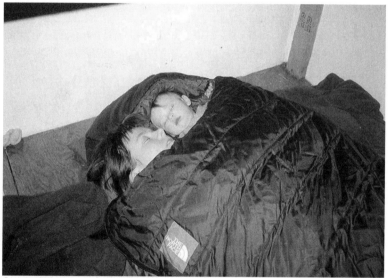

Snug against you, your baby will be nice and warm on even the coldest of nights.. [JEN AIST]

SAFETY

"It seems to be a commonly held belief that wilderness tripping is a risky business in which you leave the comforts of civilization and go out to battle the elements. The boring truth of the matter is that with proper preparation, wilderness travel is no more dangerous than a trip to the shopping mall."

—Rolf and Debra Kraiker, *Cradle to Canoe*

When going on outdoor adventures, the temptation for many is to rope off hazardous areas and create a "safe" zone for their children. But never for a moment think that you can childproof the wilderness. It can't be done.

What's more, it *shouldn't* be done. Children learn to safely interact with wild places by interacting with them. Even toddlers. Even crawling infants. I'm not proposing that parents go and take a nap, leaving the kids to fend for themselves. I'm merely suggesting that we need to back off a bit and let our kids explore.

If this concept makes you nervous, consider this: When parents constantly hover over their children, reminding them to "pay attention," "be careful," or "watch out," the children learn that their environment will always be safe because someone will always be there to let them know otherwise. These children don't learn the skills necessary to judge a dangerous situation and either stay away from it or get safely out of it.

Still doubting me? Watch an eight-month-old baby crawl around a coffee table. If left to explore it on his own, he'll run into it a few times, bonk his head on the bottom of it as he tries to crawl under it, and maybe even get a bit frustrated with it. Very quickly, this same baby will learn to duck going under that coffee table, slow down to avoid crashing into it, and generally learn how to be safe around it. The baby with "hover parents" never has an opportunity to learn by trial and error. So though this baby may never bonk his head on the coffee table at home, he also never develops the skills to avoid bonking his head on any other coffee table. Teach children the skills they need to safely negotiate any coffee table they may ever encounter, and you have given your children an incredible gift. You will have taught your child to be capable.

Remember, frustration teaches children problem solving. Boredom teaches children creativity.

Again, I am not suggesting that children do not need to be supervised. I am suggesting that we as parents need to let them make some mistakes. Babies shouldn't be permitted to eat rocks, but you don't need to rush off to stop toddlers from stomping in puddles. Skinned knees are OK. Dirty clothes are OK. Dr. Glen Austin, a longtime pediatrician and author, once told me the sign of a healthy child is one with a lot of bruises on the knees and dirt on the pants. This, he said, is the sign of an active child who is getting a lot of good playtime.

Aside from giving their children room to learn on their own, parents should model safe behavior for them.

A shallow pond is the perfect place to practice jumping. [TOM TWIGG]

A young baby enjoys the simple pleasure of crawling in wet sand. [SARAH GROSSHUESCH]

When young children see their parents wearing bike helmets, they will too. Talk to your children from birth about being safe and respectful of their bodies.

Above all, remember that keeping our children safe is a process, not a destination. It is a journey of empowering our children to make good, safe choices.

SAFETY TIP

Safety talks should not be limited to just before trips but, rather, interwoven into daily life so that children grow up learning how to be safe in all areas of their lives.

STAYING TOGETHER

Nothing can strike fear in parents quite like the idea of becoming separated from their children. Seven out of ten children will become lost at some point in their lives—but the most common place children get lost is not in the woods; it's in the mall. Practice some trail smarts to keep everyone together.

Trip plans are important to complete *before* you leave on your trip. Don't wing it when you're going on an outdoor adventure—even if it is just an afternoon hike. Let someone know where you are going, who is with you, what time you're leaving, and when you anticipate returning home. My husband and I are both members of Alaska Search and Rescue Dogs, and we can't stress enough the importance of a trip plan. It really makes a big difference for rescuers, should you need them. It doesn't need to be an elaborate plan, just these basics:

- Destination
- Number in your party; names and ages
- Departure time and date
- Anticipated return time and date
- Vehicle make and license number

At the trailhead, review the following rules of the trail:

- Stay together as a group. Always stay within speaking range on the trail. If you have to shout to be heard, you are too far apart from each other.
- Never wander away from camp or the trail without a grown-up.
- If you do get separated from your group, hug a tree. (See next section.)

SAFETY TIP

Lost children tend to travel downhill. According to the National Association of Search and Rescue, children ages one to three years wander aimlessly in a down-hill direction and seek out the most convenient location to lie down and sleep.

Hug a Tree

The National Association of Search and Rescue (NASAR) coordinates training instructors for the Hug-a-Tree and Survive Program. This program for young children is designed to teach them what to do if they get lost in the woods. Contact your local officials to see if there are trainers in your area who can present to preschools, youth groups, or schools. NASAR also has Hug-a-Tree coloring books on their web site (see Resources). The principles of Hug-a-Tree include the following tips for kids:

- Hug a tree once you know you are lost. (This reminds children to stay put instead of continuing to wander and can offer some comfort to the child.)
- Carry a trash bag and a whistle with you. (The trash bag can be used as an emergency outer layer to keep the child warm and dry; the whistle is a handy signaling device.)
- Know that your parents won't be angry that you got lost. They'll be worried and very happy to have you safe in their arms again.
- Make yourself big. (Bright colors are more easily spotted by rescuers. Likewise, hugging a tree in an open field is more visible than a tree in a dense forest.)
- You will have many friends out there looking for you.

SAFETY TIP

Searchers frequently pass by missing children while calling out their names because parents have taught their children not to go to strangers. Teach your children to signal their location by blowing a whistle or calling out if they're lost, and let them know that searchers are safe strangers trying to help them find you.

WILDERNESS FIRST AID

Although this section will help you with minor injuries on the trail, nothing can replace the skills you learn in a live Wilderness First Responder course or one like it. Standard first-aid classes assume immediate access to advanced medical care; wilderness first-aid courses teach you how to handle emergencies when advanced care is not readily available. Anyone who spends time in the backcountry can benefit from these classes. They are offered throughout the country and are typically about eighty hours long.

Bumps and Bruises

Children don't have to be out on a trail to get bumps and bruises; whether at home or outdoors, these can easily be treated with hugs and kisses and a bit of arnica gel. Arnica works by stimulating the body's own natural healing processes. It fosters the reabsorption of blood around the injury site, thus reducing swelling and bruising. Arnica comes in a stick like a lip gloss, as a gel, or as homeopathic tablets. Apply arnica immediately when a bump occurs and as frequently as needed thereafter. There are no known contraindications to arnica use in its homeopathic form. All ages—including infants—can use the topical form. My older children tell me it works better than ibuprofen on muscle soreness; as black belts in tae kwon do, they know about muscle pain!

Scrapes and Wounds

Treatment for minor scrapes, lacerations, or puncture wounds are all basically the same: clean the wound, dress it, and keep it covered. These are the foundations of good wound care.

Sick Campers

Unfortunately, either you or your children might fall ill during a trip. If you're car camping, you can just go home. Our friends Mark and Sarah were car camping with us when their two-year-old niece became ill in the middle of the night. She vomited all over their tent and sleeping bags. Dripping with vomit, they decided to pack it up. By the time the rest of us woke up in the morning, they were long gone. Sarah later told me they had never packed up so fast in all their years of camping. Nothing like a bit of puke to really get you moving.

Of course, this kind of evacuation isn't so easy if you are two days into a backcountry trip. Depending on your location and the severity of the illness, you might have to hike out quickly or even call for medical evacuation.

Here are some helpful guidelines for avoiding sickness and for coping with it if it happens:

Don't go if someone isn't feeling well. Like so many things in life, prevention is your best cure. Don't

ESSENTIAL GEAR CHECK
A Child's Ten Essentials

1. map if they're old enough to use one; otherwise, name of parents or adults in the group
2. sunglasses and sunscreen
3. extra layer of clothing
4. headlamp or flashlight
5. small first-aid kit of adhesive bandages (if your children are older than three, let them carry their own bandages)
6. whistle for signaling
7. something bright (a windbreaker or bandanna) that's easy to see
8. emergency snack (I let my kids carry a special treat like fruit snacks in their packs; I tell them they can eat them whenever they want, but they get only one package. You would be amazed at how well they ration their treats by themselves. Children as young as three can do this.)
9. treated water
10. trash bag for emergency shelter

take kids who are on the brink of illness into the backcountry. And don't go yourself if you feel something coming on. Stay home.

Wash hands. Hand washing is your single best defense against most illnesses. Although you won't have access to a sink with clean running water in the backcountry, you can still practice regular hand washing (see the Dirt chapter). At the very least, use alcohol-based hand gel before eating and after diapering and toileting. Whenever possible, heat up some water on the stove and wash hands and faces thoroughly.

Treat drinking water. Make certain you have treated drinking water properly. This is especially important with infants and absolutely critical with formula-fed infants. See "Purifying Water" in the Food chapter.

Stay hydrated. If anyone in your party falls ill and going home isn't an immediate option, do your best to keep the person comfortable and reduce cross contamination. Whether symptoms are vomiting or diarrhea, your enemy is dehydration. Push fluids as much as possible. If your baby or toddler is still breastfeeding, feed him or her frequently.

WILD FACT
Don't Get Burned

The number-one injury among people who travel in the backcountry is burns.

Burns

In the outdoors, burns can happen from a variety of sources, including stoves, fires, sun, matches, and lighters. Make it your practice to never lay down your lighter or matches; always keep a hand on them or store them in your pocket. If you have a campfire, designate an adult to be on patrol. Tripping and falling into a fire is all too easy for a toddler or preschooler.

Treat burns by cleaning them with lukewarm water and mild soap, pat dry, and apply a loose dressing. Get to a doctor as soon as possible.

Broken Bones

Broken bones require medical attention. Doctors say that parents frequently mistake fractures for sprains. When in doubt, treat an injury as if it is a broken bone: stabilize the injury as much as possible and get to the doctor.

First-Aid Kits

Put together some first-aid kits at home by following these three steps:
1. Assemble items such as gauze pads and bandages (see Checklists).
2. Write the date you made the kit and its contents on a slip of paper. This will make it easier to find what you need and update the items later.

3. Put all of these items together in a sealable plastic pouch and seal it. Use a vacuum sealer to suck out all the air, making the kit very compact and watertight. These skinny first-aid kits can fit almost anywhere in your pack.

Some families fill antibiotics prescriptions before they head out on trips. If you plan to be out of reach from medical help for extended periods, this isn't a bad idea. Make sure you discuss with your pediatrician the age when it is appropriate to begin antibiotic therapy for your child.

> ## TIPS & TRICKS
>
> Effective emergency splints can be made from all sorts of items you probably have with you:
> - T-shirts can be used as bandaging.
> - Closed-cell sleep pads can serve as splints.
> - Cold lake water can serve as an ice bath.

LIGHTNING

Know the weather patterns of the area you plan to visit. For example, in mountainous areas, thunderstorms typically develop in the early afternoon, so plan to hike early in the day and be down the mountain by noon. Know the weather forecast for the time you will be in that area. If there is a high chance of thunderstorms, curtail your outdoor activities there, or go to another location.

I remember visiting family in Kansas when I was a kid, and an afternoon thunderstorm came roaring across the prairie. There was thunder, lightning, hail, and wind. We were visiting from California, and my sister and I had never

A baby carrier can serve as a sling if you need to stabilize a broken arm for a short time. [JEN AIST]

seen such a sight. We immediately ran out to the screen porch to watch the show. We weren't there but a minute when our aunt snatched us up and ran us straight down to the basement. The Kansans in the room looked at us as though we were crazy loons, wanting to watch a storm like that. We learned our lesson that day. As the National Weather Service (NWS) says, "When thunder roars, go indoors!" And if you are in tornado country, head for the basement.

If thunderstorms are forecast or likely, do not place your campsite in an open field on the top of a hill or on a ridge top. Keep your site away from isolated tall trees or other tall objects. If you are in a forest, stay near a lower stand of trees. If you are camping in an open area, set up camp in a valley, ravine, or other low area. A tent offers no protection from lightning.

During a lightning storm, no place is 100 percent safe, but some locations are safer than others. If you can possibly run to a vehicle or enclosed building, do so. Sitting or crouching on the ground is not safe, just a last resort if an enclosed building or vehicle is not available. Picnic shelters and tents are not considered safe. If you're car camping, your best bet is to get into your car, even if that means walking some distance to get to it. The car must be enclosed to be considered safe, so convertibles aren't safe, even with the top up (unless it is a metal top—canvas tops offer no protection). Wait thirty minutes after you last hear thunder to come back out of the car.

If lightning is in the immediate area, and there is no safe location nearby, stay at least fifteen feet apart from other members of your group so the lightning won't travel between you if someone is hit. If you are not near a safe location, NWS gives the following advice to lessen your odds of being hit by lightning:

- Do *not* seek shelter under isolated tall trees. The tree may help you stay dry but will significantly increase your risk of being struck by lightning. Rain will not kill you, but lightning can.
- Do *not* seek shelter under partially enclosed buildings such as picnic shelters.
- Stay away from isolated tall objects. Lightning typically strikes the tallest object, which might be *you* in an open field or clearing.
- Stay away from metal objects such as fences, poles, umbrellas, and backpacks. Metal is an excellent conductor of electricity.

Wet ropes can also make excellent conductors, which is bad news when there's lightning. If you are mountain climbing and see lightning, remove unnecessary ropes extended or attached to you, if you can do so safely. If a rope is extended across the mountain face and lightning makes contact with it, the electrical current will likely travel along the rope, especially if it's wet.

For other hazards from natural phenomena, see the Clothing and Sun chapters.

WILDLIFE

Teach your children to be aware of wild creatures in their environment. Teach

WILD FACT
Lightning Strikes

The current from a lightning flash will easily travel for long distances, up to a mile or more.

them to respect the power and intelligence of these animals. Don't teach them to be fearful that they will be attacked on every hike. Teach them the skills necessary to avoid a confrontation as well as the skills to survive an encounter.

Snakes

Snakes generally have a bad rap, but they really are cool animals. They are extremely helpful at keeping rodent populations in check and are amazing predators to watch in action. Of the many species of snakes that live across the United States, only four are poisonous: rattlesnakes, coral snakes, cottonmouths, and copperheads. Believe it or not, snakes really do want to avoid humans. Some common sense on your part will keep everyone safe and happy:

- Never put your hands or feet where you can't see them.
- When you know you're in snake country, wear boots that cover your ankles and loose long pants to protect yourself from bites.
- Don't set up your tent in tall grass, where snakes like to hang out.
- If there's any chance the snake is a rattler, skedaddle as soon as you see it.

Keep in mind that snake bites are rare, and fewer than a dozen individuals die each year from snake bites. If a snake does bite you or your child, remember the following:

- Do *not* use ice to cool the bite.
- Do *not* cut open the wound and try to suck out the venom.
- Do *not* use a tourniquet.
- Do wash the bite with soap and water.
- Do immobilize the bitten area and keep the wound lower than the heart.
- Do get medical help immediately.

Bears, Cougars, and Other Large Animals

While there are numerous stories about big animals such as bears, cougars, and other predators attacking humans, in reality this is rare. Attacks occur when animals are surprised or when you come between a mother and her baby or an animal and its kill.

You can reduce your chances of an encounter with a large predator by avoiding these situations and taking some simple precautions:

- Keep a clean camp. Follow local guidelines regarding food storage at campsites.
- Travel in groups. There has not been a recorded bear attack on a group of four or more people, and other large animals are more likely to leave you alone in a large group as well.
- Pay attention to animal signs along the trail. Tracks and scat will give you clues about recent activity. Many trails have signs posted at the trailhead about recent sightings.
- Make noise along the trail. Although this is pretty well guaranteed when young children are in the group, hanging bear bells on your pack or singing helps to alert bears, moose, or elk of your presence and gives the animal a chance to move out of the way.
- If your canine "child" is hiking with you, keep him or her on a leash. Many dogs wander ahead and lead bears back to their group.

A young moose family checks out the play equipment at a campground. [KARIN BRAUN]

If you do have an encounter with a large animal in the wild, make sure you know how to respond:

- Whether it is a black bear or brown bear, moose or elk, cougar or wolf, if the animal is standing its ground and checking you out from a distance, make yourself look big—wave your arms, stand in a big group. Keep your babies and toddlers right beside you.
- If a bear charges you, stand your ground unless and until the bear actually touches you. Then drop flat to the ground with your child under you, dig your toes in, wrap your arms behind your head, and play dead. If an elk or moose charges you, drop to the ground immediately.
- If a cougar or wolf charges you, fight back aggressively.

Though this all sounds very frightening, remember that such attacks actually are rare and that you now know what to do should you have an encounter. Don't let a fear of wild animals keep you from getting out there.

SAFETY TIP

Many people feel passionately, one way or the other, about guns, especially when it comes to bringing them into the backcountry. One of the reasons I don't recommend bringing along a gun is that it can give you a false sense of security. You may not be as careful about keeping a clean camp if you think that the gun is your ultimate protection from wildlife.

I live in Alaska, where the vast majority of households own guns. And I see many reports of children accidentally shooting themselves and each other with loaded guns. Loaded guns and young children are a terrible combination. If you must bring a gun along on an outdoor outing with children, please do the following:

- Make sure you really know how to use the gun.
- Make sure it is an appropriate gun for the habitat you're visiting.
- Camp and hike as if you have honey smeared all over you and you don't have a gun along.
- Make sure the gun is never unattended—ever.

PART II

Transporting Little Ones on the Trail

**Child Carriers | Jogging Strollers |
Bike Trailers, Trailer Bikes, and Bikes**

CHILD CARRIERS

"Baby wearing equals keeping your baby happy plus getting on with your life."

—The BabyWearer.com

Historians say that child carriers were probably the first tools ever made by humankind—we just don't have any record of them because they were made from hide or some other natural material that didn't survive through the ages. Mothers have always needed to carry out their daily chores with a baby or young child in tow. Slings, cradleboards, wraps, and more have filled the bill for thousands and thousands of years.

I started baby wearing with my first child, not because I'd read about it or because I knew others who were doing it, but for the oldest reason there is: necessity. I carried my daughter because I had to go back to work and wanted her with me.

Baby wearing is just a fancy term that means carrying your baby or young child. Baby wearing is not defined by the type of carrier you use or the amount of hours you do it per day. Baby wearing isn't a social movement; it is simply a means of having your hands free with your baby on your body. Since hiking and camping with babies involves a significant amount of time carrying them, it is important to discuss concerns about and benefits of baby wearing.

Concerns About Baby Wearing

Parents ask me if it is harmful to carry their babies. They bring up concerns such as spoiling their baby, hampering motor development or independence, straining mama's back, and sacrificing "kid-free time" for mom. What research tells us about baby wearing is almost universally positive; however, there are some valid concerns.

Certainly, some carriers are easier on your back than others. Most physical therapists I know cringe when they hear about someone carrying a baby all day long. Having carried babies for more than ten years straight, I have to agree with their concern. It isn't the nicest thing to do to your back. However, you can mitigate this impact (see "Carrying Babies Safely and Comfortably" later in this chapter).

Some carriers support babies in a way that can hamper their circulation and negatively impact development of their hips. See the chart later in this chapter for products that avoid these problems.

Every now and then, I hear about a baby who suffocated in a baby carrier. Some of these deaths happened because the parent had the baby zipped into their coat in cold weather in such a way that didn't allow for good oxygen

Around camp, you will be carrying your baby a lot. [JEN AIST]

flow. There also have been some cases of babies coming close to suffocation when they got wedged down low in a sling with their chin smooshed up against their chest. See "Carrying Babies Safely and Comfortably" later in this chapter, for tips on avoiding these hazards.

Finally, some babies have been injured in carriers while their parents participated in activities such as skiing downhill, operating a chain saw, or using small blowtorches. Use some common sense to avoid these dangers.

Benefits of Baby Wearing

Are these concerns outweighed by the benefits of baby wearing? Let's take a look:

- **Carried babies cry less.** Several studies (such as in *Pediatrics*, Vol. 77 No. 5 May 1986, pages 641–648) have shown that three hours of baby wearing a day amounts to 43 percent less crying.
- **Carrying babies is convenient.** Let's face it; babies want to be held. You either figure out how to do that while you get on with your life, or you go crazy.

- **Carrying babies enhances their brain development.** When babies are content or in a quiet alert state, brain development flourishes. When they are stressed or crying, babies go into a flight or fight hormonal state with stress hormones dominant in the bloodstream. In this state of stress, the brain is not able to engage in active learning.
- **Carrying babies enhances their emotional development.** The primary goal of infancy is for a baby to establish a sense of trust. When a baby's needs are met and the baby feels secure, trust ensues. Responding promptly to a baby's cues fosters a strong sense of independence in that baby. The only way to spoil a baby is the same way you spoil fruit: leaving it to rot on the counter.
- **Carrying babies enhances their motor development.** Babies who are carried have a better sense of balance and enhanced depth perception. Because they are constantly in motion, they get lots of practice adjusting their equilibrium to being up and down and all around. Moving toward and away from objects fosters development of depth perception. They see a tree as small in the distance, then watch it get bigger as they move toward it. Interestingly, babies who are exclusively carried roll over, crawl, and walk at the same time as babies who have more floor time.
- **Carrying babies enhances their language development.** Babies learn language by hearing it. Infant babble—the noises babies make as they're developing language—is universal for the first three months of life. After three months, the brain begins to selectively pare down connections in the language center to only those the baby will need to speak in his or her environment. Many people talking to your baby—a more likely occurrence in a carrier than a stroller—increases your baby's exposure to language and vocabulary.

CARRYING BABIES SAFELY AND COMFORTABLY

I am a big fan of baby wearing. I carried my kids all day long for fifteen months apiece. Well, I didn't actually carry both twins all the time—there *is* a limit! My kids were totally accustomed to being in a pouch on my front, side, or back. They thrived on the closeness, the noise, and the constant bumps along the road. Here are some suggestions I've learned through the years to ensure safe and comfortable baby wearing.

Tips for Parents

Get your abs in good shape. A strong core goes far in supporting both moms' and dads' backs. I don't like sit-ups any more than the next person, but they really do make a difference. You will be a happier camper if you have a strong back that doesn't hurt.

New moms should look for classes that cater to the postpartum condition. Your transformed body has special needs that require an instructor who knows his or her stuff. Be especially careful if you are recovering from a cesarean birth. Don't start out with crunches. Beginner exercises after a cesarean consist of just sliding your foot up and down the bed while you're lying on your back. Advanced exercises include sitting up straight in a chair, tightening your abdominal muscles, and leaning back slightly. It takes time, but your abs will get back in shape. Dads, on the other hand, have a green light for doing abdominal exercises right away.

Positioning Your Baby

Oxygen is a beautiful thing. Always make sure your baby can freely breathe. The baby's chin should be slightly flexed. Maternity centers talk about placing the baby's face in the "sniffing" position: the nose slightly angled up, as if sniffing a flower. This ensures a nice, open airway. If the baby's chin is wedged down on his or her chest, the airway is compromised. Reposition the baby.

If you are trying to cover your baby in cold or sunny conditions, make absolutely sure that there is a path for fresh air. Parents tell me all the time that they put a blanket

A buckle carrier can be worn on the front or back. [LARISSA WRIGHT-ELSON]

over the baby's face so he or she will sleep better. The baby sleeps more because he or she isn't getting enough fresh oxygen! Rebreathing the same air is dangerous. Don't cover up babies.

Choosing a Child Carrier

Dozens of different baby carriers are on the market today, from soft-structured carriers to wraps, slings, and external-frame carriers. Some are better than others. The accompanying chart covers some points to consider when you're deciding which one to use while hiking.

CARRIER TYPE	FEATURES	ADVANTAGES	DISADVANTAGES
Baby Bjorn	These soft-structured carriers come in a few versions of the same basic style, which consists of lightly padded straps that crisscross on the parent's back and suspend the baby's weight from his or her crotch. Many parents swear by the back support versions. These are probably the most popular baby carriers on the market.	Shoulder straps lie flat, allowing a backpack to fit nicely over it. The material is tightly woven and doesn't absorb rain as much as some other carriers. The baby can face toward you or away from you. You can wear two for twins, if needed.	Suspends the baby's weight totally from the baby's crotch, which leads to poor circulation in the baby's legs and does *not* provide the baby with optimal hip support. Designed to be worn only on the front of the parent. Fits babies only to a maximum of one year old. Most babies grow out of them at around six months old because their legs are too long to hang straight down anymore. Really difficult to walk uphill or up stairs because the baby's feet stand on your thighs.
Ergo	A soft-structured carrier with padded shoulder straps. The baby's weight is suspended from his or her hips, not the crotch.	Available in organic materials. Fits newborns to older toddlers well. Has a newborn insert ideal for tiny babies. Can be worn on the front or the back of the parent. Lots of parents swear by its comfort. Comes with detachable pouches and fanny packs for more storage. An attached hood can be pulled up over a sleeping child.	Most models are made of 100 percent cotton, which takes a while to dry. A cotton-polyester sport model is better suited for the outdoors. The straps are pretty thick, so it is difficult, but not impossible, to wear a backpack over it.

CARRIER TYPE	FEATURES	ADVANTAGES	DISADVANTAGES
Mei Tai	Traditional Asian soft-structured baby carrier that distributes the baby's weight evenly over both your shoulders and ties behind your back or in the front. Baby's weight is suspended from his or her hips.	Can be worn on the front or back. Fits small infants to toddlers.	The tie knots can be very uncomfortable under a backpack.
Soft-structured buckle carrier	Similar in design to the Mei Tai, but with buckles instead of ties. The baby's weight is suspended from his or her hips, with light support on the sides.	Buckles eliminate bulky knots that are uncomfortable under a backpack. Most have nice head support for the baby in the proper sitting position, as well as sleeping babies or toddlers.	Generally made of cotton, which doesn't weather well.
Wrap	Approximately five yards of material that you wrap around your body in different ways and tie off the ends.	Can be worn in a variety of ways, on the front or the back. Fits newborns, twins, even four-year-olds. Depending on how you use the wrap, you can wear a backpack over it. Provides great head support for young babies. Some are made of cotton knit; Moby makes one with UPF 50-rated fabric. You can easily wear a large raincoat over it.	Dries very slowly after rain exposure, due to the amount of material, though non-cotton wraps dry quicker.
Pouch sling or ring sling	A pocket of fabric for the baby to sit in; it goes over just one of your shoulders. A ring sling has two metal rings that lock the fabric into place.	Easy to use and extremely versatile. Comes in a variety of materials, including fleece for cooler weather. Fits newborns to pre-schoolers. You can wear two slings for twins, one over each shoulder.	A ring sling's fabric bulk on one shoulder makes wearing a backpack over it very uncomfortable. Does not offer a lot of support to either the baby or the parent on bumpy terrain.
External-frame backpack	Highly structured carriers that often have similar suspension systems to traditional backpacks and come with storage pouches for extra gear.	Easy to attach backpacking gear onto the frame. Less confining space for the baby. Generally made from nylon, which weathers well. Rain covers and sunshades are readily available.	Often a 2-inch gap between your back and where the child sits, which puts a lot of strain on your back. The baby's weight is suspended mostly from the crotch, similarly to the Baby Bjorn.

Consider some other factors as well before purchasing a carrier. Does it fit both parents? Some carriers can cost $100 or more, so purchasing one for each parent isn't always an option.

How does the carrier feel on your body? Fitting baby backpacks and carriers is exactly the same as fitting any other pack. Take the time to fit your pack the best you can. It will make a big difference for your back.

If you are trying on a carrier at a store, put your baby in it and walk around the store for at least an hour. Go up and down stairs if the store has them. Lean over, twist, and turn. Really put that carrier through the wringer. Attach a sleep pad, a camp stove, and a sleeping bag to it. Find out what it can really carry.

TIPS & TRICKS

Many communities have baby wearing groups with "lending libraries" of carriers you can check out for a week or so to help you learn how to use the various carriers and decide which one you really like before you commit to a purchase.

An older child enjoys carrying a baby in a wrap. [AMELIA OLIVER]

You might also consider a baby-wearing coat, which has conveniently located holes for little heads to poke out. These coats are cut generously to allow for the baby to fit under it. These garments are available as vests, raincoats, winter jackets, and parkas. Some will even accommodate twins or two children.

WILD FACT
Marsupials

Once opossum babies are too big for their mom's pouch, they climb onto her back, where she continues to carry them until they are too big.

GIVING LITTLE LIFTS TO TODDLERS AND PRESCHOOLERS

Babies need to be carried all the time, but at some point your little camper will be able to take to the trail him- or herself, at least part of the time. Then you need to carry little ones just when they need a little lift. Always have a system ready to carry any child younger than five, even if they are great hikers.

This pack fits well; notice how close the baby is to her dad's back. Some carriers position the baby too far from the parent, which puts extra strain on the back. [SHAD O'NEEL]

Slings

You likely won't want to bring a baby backpack (or a jogging stroller) if the toddler needs to be carried (or pushed) only periodically. Slings can work nicely, since they don't take up very much room in your pack, and they are also easy to put on and take off. Toddlers can be carried in a sling on your hip or your back, but if you're carrying a toddler on your back, you can't wear your day pack or backpack. This is no big deal if you are hiking with someone else who can carry your gear.

Fanny Packs

If you're traveling alone or if no one else can carry your pack, consider using a fanny pack instead of a backpack for your gear. Some fabulous fanny packs on the market right now can accommodate a generous amount of gear, and some even have shoulder straps to help with the load. Kids in slings can be carried in any position while you're wearing a fanny pack.

My favorite carrying method for a toddler or preschooler is to have the child sit on top of my fanny pack. If the child falls asleep, I tie my sweatshirt around him or her to secure the child

This day pack does double duty with a zipout child-carrier section. [DAWN ANDERSON]

A Mei Tai can be worn on the parent's front or back. [SARAH GROSSHUESCH]

to my back, tying the sweatshirt arms in a knot across my chest. Children as young as eighteen months can be carried this way for short periods.

Backpacks

When I'm backpacking and need to carry a child for a bit, I shift the top lid of my pack back a little bit. This creates room for a nice seat on my shoulders for the weary toddler. When I need to change positions, I switch the toddler to sitting on my fanny pack on my front. The fanny pack can be shifted to one hip or my front to spread the weight around.

Another option is a combination child carrier–day pack: basically, a small day pack with a child carrier zipped into it. When you aren't carrying a child, you can zip up the seat to keep it out of the way. While these packs don't offer great back support for the parent, they are certainly handy for the occasional rider.

JOGGING STROLLERS

"The most indispensable piece of baby gear we ever bought?
Definitely the double jogging stroller."

—Corey Aist's advice to new parents

ow can a *jogging stroller* change your life? Four children later, I know the answer: mobility. True, strollers make you mobile, but jogging strollers, with their off-road capabilities, give you a greater choice of trails. Not all toddlers and preschoolers want to walk or be carried, so a jogging stroller is the perfect ticket to get these kids out on the trail with the family.

Baby joggers are the best thing to happen to strollers since strollers became collapsible. The fundamental difference between a jogger and a conventional stroller is the wheels. Joggers have three wheels—not four—with large, usually inflatable tires. Some have a fixed front wheel, while others have a front wheel that can be fixed or released to turn freely. Some baby joggers even accommodate an infant car seat. Joggers are generally quite a bit bigger than traditional strollers.

Being mobile is powerful. I already had two children under the age of five when our twins were born. I know women with even more kids, but I was feeling pretty maxed out with four. My house felt like it was getting smaller by the day, and with winter setting in, I knew it would only get smaller. I had to figure out a way to get outside with two newborns and two preschoolers. I couldn't carry both babies for long, especially if the three-year-old decided he needed a lift.

This is how the stroller changed my life: I was able to put the twins in the seats, and my three-year-old could ride on the foot rest while the five-year-old helped me push. There was plenty of room underneath for snacks and drinks. Suddenly it became possible to walk around the block and get back on the trails. We all got much-needed fresh air and a break from our everyday routines. I was able to get some exercise to recover from pregnancy and a cesarean birth. I felt invincible with my babies strapped in and ready to go. My stroller became an extension of my body for a long time.

CHOOSING A JOGGING STROLLER

Jogging strollers are expensive, so it is important to research your dream rig before you buy. The following chart gives some points to consider.

An increasing number of companies are making multi-use strollers that convert to bike trailers, strollers, and jogging strollers. These are a great option if you are considering buying the other items anyway.

There is a fabulous infant sling attachment for use with a jogging stroller that supports a young baby's head and neck well with a three-point harness. The manufacturer (Chariot) advises that you not use it to bike with little babies.

Jogging strollers can hold quite a bit of gear on the trail. [JEN AIST]

Young babies need extra support in jogging strollers, as the sling attachment shown here provides. [SARAH FINEMAN]

TRAVELING THE TRAIL

Once you have your rig, it's time to hit the trails. Generally speaking, if the trail is accessible to bikes, it will work for a single jogging stroller. Ask other parents who have used a trail about its width. Any handicap-accessible trail is great for a single or double jogging stroller. The ideal jogger-friendly trail will have these features:

- Be wide enough to accommodate the jogging stroller
- Not have any river crossings
- Not have too many big rocks or roots to navigate (bumpy trails aren't very comfortable for the child; heads get bumped around a lot)
- Have a gentle grade—a trail that rarely exceeds a 10 percent grade is ideal

QUESTIONS TO ASK	FEATURES TO LOOK FOR
1. How old is your child? Are you planning on having more babies? How many years do you plan to use the stroller?	**Infants.** Babies less than one year of age—and especially younger than six months of age—really need a seat that reclines. Most don't recline flat, which is OK—they don't need to be completely flat. Some seats are really a nuisance to recline. Still others are impossible to recline without waking the sleeping child inside. Don't buy one that can't be easily and smoothly reclined, preferably with one hand. **Toddlers.** If your youngest is fifteen months or older and you aren't planning on having any more babies, the reclining feature isn't as important. However, the five-point harness is more important than it is for a young baby. As your child develops the strength and will to get out of the stroller while you are cruising down the trail, you will appreciate the five-point system even more. **Preschoolers.** Jogging strollers are great until your child is about three or four years old. After that, the child is too heavy and too tall to fit comfortably in it, and it becomes too hard for you to steer. Keep this in mind before you spend a lot of money.
2. How many kids will be riding in it?	**Singleton.** Get a single stroller. **Twins.** You need a double-wide. With a couple of exceptions, double joggers are side by side. Pushing one feels similar to driving a barge, but just remember the incredible upper-body strength you'll gain. **Two siblings of varying ages.** If the two children are at least two years apart in age, you may be able to just use a single, first for the older child, then later for the younger. An older sibling who occasionally needs a ride can sit on the footrest. This won't work on all stroller models, so look closely at the footrest to determine its flexibility and function. If the two children are less than two years apart in age, use a double jogger.

QUESTIONS TO ASK	FEATURES TO LOOK FOR
3. What are you going to use it for?	**Walking downtown.** You'll need a more compact model to navigate sidewalks as well as trails. **Jogging or running.** For speeds faster than a stroll, the leash is an important safety feature. Some parents like to have a hand-brake system as well, but most don't use it. **Backpacking.** You want a strong chassis that can handle large quantities of gear strapped to it. Ask yourself these questions: Where will I attach sleeping pads and sleeping bags? Can the sunshade support any weight on top of it? Will my baby or toddler be comfortable in it for extended periods?
4. What kind of surface are you planning on using it on?	**Mostly paved or nearly paved trails.** Wheel size isn't as important as turning power; look for a stroller that has the option of locking the front wheel or leaving it free to rotate. If you will be hauling it in your car, check how easily it collapses and whether it will fit in your trunk. **Mostly unpaved trails.** Look more closely at how the jogger is built. Off-road trails with roots and rocks put a lot of torque on the stroller's joints. Don't buy a model that uses just a cotter pin to hold it together; these tend to pop out with enough wear and tear, posing a danger to your child. Cantilevered wheels provide more stability. Look closely at how the child is held into the seat; a five-point harness is a must-have. The sides where the child's head could bump should be well padded. The whole seat should swing, to minimize jolts on the trail and avoid shaken-baby syndrome.
5. What kind of conditions will you be using it in?	**Hot and sunny.** In hot and sunny climes, you need a sunshade. Look for one that comes all the way in front of the baby. You can also purchase attachments made out of UPF fabric to provide additional shading. **Rainy.** In wet areas, you need a really solid rain shield. Make sure it covers the footrest and back side of the stroller entirely.

BIKE TRAILERS, TRAILER BIKES, AND BIKES

"The bicycle is a curious vehicle. Its passenger is its engine."

—John Howard

hat do bikes and bike trailers have to do with taking babies into the woods? Plenty, especially when those babies are too big to carry but too small to walk far or fast themselves. Like jogging strollers, bikes and bike trailers can open up miles of trails and a multitude of camping opportunities. Whether you're pulling a bike trailer or a trailer bike or riding alongside your blossoming rider, bikes can be a great way to get deeper into wilderness areas. Welcome to the wonderful world of "bike hiking"!

No matter which type of bicycle conveyance you use with your children, be sure to bring along your repair kit, so that you're prepared for a flat tire or other minor mishaps.

PROTECTING LITTLE HEADS

Manufacturers of bike trailers and helmets recommend that you do *not* use them until your baby is at least one year of age. The smallest bike helmet on the market is sized for a one year old.

Never, *ever* put a baby younger than one year of age in a carrier seat on a bike post. The baby's musculature and bone structure are not strong enough to support him or her in the upright sitting position such a seat demands. And when the child falls asleep, all the weight of the baby's head and helmet is thrust forward, greatly compromising the baby's airway.

Babies less than one year old shouldn't go biking in trailers either. Biking creates a lot of bounce for the child—much more than you might think. Remember that your baby is sitting right over the bike trailer's wheels, and there just isn't anything else to absorb the jostling except for the baby. Your young baby is at risk for shaken-baby syndrome when riding in a bike trailer if he or she is younger than one year of age.

If you are curious about just how much force it takes to cause brain damage via shaken-baby syndrome, do the following experiment: Crack a fresh egg open into a clear jar. Now shake it. When the yolk goes *splat* in the jar, you have the equivalent of traumatic brain injury.

Helmets

Helmets are essential equipment for all bikers. Yes, that includes mom and dad, too. According to Safe Kids USA, properly fitted bike helmets could reduce the risk of bike-related brain injuries by 88 percent. Helmets could prevent up to 45,000 head injuries to children each year. Make wearing helmets a family thing.

Safe Kids USA offers the following advice for fitting helmets on children:
- The helmet should sit on the top of the child's head in a level position.
- The helmet should not rock forward and backward or side to side.
- The helmet straps must always be buckled snugly.

Do a quick "eyes, ears, and mouth" test before heading out: The helmet rim should be just above the eyebrows. The helmet straps should form a V around the child's ear-lobes. The buckle should be flat and snug against the skin under the chin.

BIKE TRAILERS

Bike trailers are much safer than the carrier seats that attach to the seat post of your bike. The trailer should attach low on the rear-wheel frame of your bike. A safety leash should secure the trailer in case the primary attachment mechanism fails. And the trailer really must have a five-point harness for its passenger. Trailers come with screens that protect your child from bugs and flying debris.

Additional features to look for include a flexible backing around the child's head, so that it can be held straight with a helmet on. Otherwise, the child's head is thrust forward due to the distance the helmet projects in the back. This is not safe; it compromises the child's airway.

Interior pockets are great for holding treasured rocks and sippy cups. Look closely at the amount of storage available. Some trailers have more legroom, and others have more storage room on the exterior back. It is probably a toss-up where you want to have more space, but I'd usually go for more legroom for the kid.

Bike trailers have a long life. Whereas bouncy chairs are good for six months, exer-saucers for four months, and most clothing for three months, you are likely to still be using your bike trailer when your "baby" enters junior high. Don't worry; you won't still be pulling your teenager! You'll find that bike trailers are also great for hauling gear. We use ours on trips to the park all the time, to carry coolers, lawn chairs, and blankets.

Starting Out

After your toddler is one year of age and outfitted with the proper helmet, start taking bike rides together. Here are some suggestions for a successful ride:

Start out on paved trails to see how your child likes it, and keep it short in the beginning. The goal is for all of you to have fun, and it isn't fun pulling a screaming toddler. Once you have figured out your and your toddler's limits, you can venture out a bit further.

Always be careful on gravel and bumpy trails. Go slow; walk your bike over big roots in the trail. While the risk of shaken-baby syndrome is highest with younger babies, it can still happen with toddlers. A trail labeled for mountain biking does not mean it is safe for young children in bike trailers.

Pack a sippy cup and some books for the ride. One mom I know packs crayons and a note pad for her toddler and preschooler to take nature notes along the ride.

Plan ahead for a sleeping child. Throw in some pillows or blankets to lean up against. Check on your child often. Pillows can really help give the child a lateral spot to rest his or her head instead of it just falling forward.

Trailer bikes give preschoolers practice balancing on a bike. [JANE HODGSON]

Always use the screen in front of the trailer. It prevents road rocks from hitting your child. It also keeps bees and mosquitoes out and provides a small amount of shading on sunny days.

TRAILER BIKES

When your child is a bit older, you can try out a trailer bike, which attaches to the seat post of your bike. This small bike has a handlebar and either one wheel or gears and two wheels.

Most children are ready for this new adventure at around three to four years old (tandem bikes are for older kids). The child has to be old enough to sit up and stay balanced while you are pedaling. The child also has to be tall enough to reach the pedals. When the child's leg is on the pedal extended down to its lowest point, the leg should be just slightly bent.

Before taking your child on a ride, go around the block a few times with the empty trailer bike. Get comfortable with the extra weight and how the trailer bike changes your balance.

Use caution with trailer bikes off-road—there is quite a bit of bounce for the child rider, and you can't see them all the time while you are riding.

A tandem bike and a trailer bike is another way to bring along two kids. [JONATHAN DITTO]

Toting More Than One Young Biker

If you want to take more than one tot along, you can. Double trailer bikes are tandem trailer bikes with two seats, two handlebars, and two sets of pedals in line with each other. A word of warning: these can be very challenging to control.

Some families attach a bike trailer behind the trailer bike. That is a lot to tow. A trailer bike attached to a tandem is another possibility.

A BIKE OF ONE'S OWN

Most kids learn to ride a two-wheeler at around age four or five. When your child is learning to ride without training wheels, it is a great idea to use a small bike from which the child can easily reach the ground with both feet. This size bike usually sports 12-inch-diameter wheels. Once your child grows more confident, move up to a bike with a larger wheelbase so he or she won't have to spin the pedals around so much to get anywhere.

TIPS & TRICKS

A plethora of youth bikes are available on the market, and some are obviously higher quality than others. Unless your budget allows, don't bother with high-end bikes for young children. They won't need them until they're older.

You probably won't be able to cover many miles biking with your child on his or her own bike until he or she is closer to eight to ten years old, so your trips will be limited to paved or really well-maintained trails. Choose relatively flat trails to help reduce crashes from riding too fast down steep hills.

When heading out on a bike ride, always have a contingency plan in case someone gets hurt or too tired to ride back. Think about towing the bike trailer just in case your little one needs a ride; I've been glad whenever I've pulled one along. The child's bike can be secured to the roof of the trailer with webbing.

Paved bike trails are perfect for new riders.
[JEN AIST]

ESSENTIAL GEAR CHECK
Biking

- bike helmet
- water bottle
- extra layers of clothes
- bike repair kit

PART III

Having Adventures

**Trip Planning | Day Hiking | Car Camping |
Base Camping | Backpacking | Boating | Exceptional Children**

TRIP PLANNING

"Are we gonna sleep in the tent or the cabin? Will there be bears?
Snakes? Can I bring all my dollies? And can I make cookies out
there?"

—Becca, age three, asking the important questions before a trip

If you read nothing else in this book, read this chapter. Planning will make or break your trip. Traveling in the backcountry with young children requires much more thought than traveling with just a partner or a group of friends. The goal of this book is to inspire families to take their kids out into the big backyard not just once but many times—and truly enjoy it. Planning and organization are the keys to making camp time a success. Once you've determined you want to take your baby or child on an outdoor adventure of some sort, the next step is to answer the questions in this chapter.

WHAT IS YOUR GOAL FOR THE TRIP?

Ask this simple question even for short day hikes. Are you going to toodle with toddlers and watch ants on the trail? Are you hoping for a workout hike? Is the goal to get to the destination? Or is the hike itself the goal?

Make sure everyone going is on the same page before you leave your house. This is critical to the success of your trip. This isn't the time to try out that major river crossing everyone has been talking about. Folks without kids don't always understand what it means to have a child along. Let them know you are on baby time now.

WHAT IS YOUR LEVEL OF EXPERIENCE?

Before setting foot on the trail, parents have to have some basic backcountry skills. You don't have to be far from the city to put yourself in a lot of potential danger. You don't need to be an Eagle Scout to take your kids out hiking, but you do need some common sense and basic skills.

Take a wilderness first-aid course. Everyone should take an annual CPR (cardiopulmonary resuscitation) course. It is the first responders—that means you—that save lives.

Know how to read a map and use a compass. Good topographical maps are readily available. Many outdoor gear stores have kiosks where you can print out zoomed-in sections of maps. These are nice when you want to bring just the section of map for your trip. Classes and books on basic map and compass skills are available everywhere, including online.

Never rely on a cell phone as your emergency plan. Don't go beyond your skill set without a trained guide with you.

With a common goal for their hike, these moms are bound to have a good time. [LIZZY DONOVAN]

SAFETY TIP

Safety gear is an investment in yourself and those you travel with. Purchase and know how to use the safety gear appropriate for your trip.

HOW OLD IS YOUR CHILD?

Needs of children vary with age, so look closely at the ages of the kids. For example, an eight year old may not want to rest as frequently or walk as slowly as a two year old will.

Young infants: birth to six months old. Generally speaking, the younger the child, the easier the trip. Babies from birth to about six months old are easy to carry and don't require heavy food, and their gear doesn't take up much space. Primarily, this age group sleeps and looks around. They are an easy-to-please crowd.

Older infants: six to fifteen months old. From six months to fifteen months old, the situation dramatically changes. Because babies this age tend to be mobile, life around camp can be challenging. You need to think about where you're going and the trail to get there to make sure your campsite won't be on a cliff or on the shores of a swift river. If you're renting a public use cabin, rent one on the ground level to avoid stairs. Remember, nothing is baby-proofed out there.

Older babies may not be as content to sit in a backpack all day either. More frequent breaks on the trail are often needed. You'll need to allow extra time to reach your destination. You'll be packing food for them, as well as more gear.

Rock climbing is a great way to build strength and confidence in children. Harnesses are made to fit children as young as three years of age.
[JANE HODGSON]

Toddlers: fifteen months to three years old. In the toddler years, trip planning changes again. Often, these children are too heavy to carry all day. That may mean that you'll need to push or pull them instead, which limits your trail choices to those that are appropriate for a jogging stroller. You'll probably want to limit the distance traveled and the duration of the trip. Consider also how long the drive to the trailhead will be. Remember, toddlers are very sensitive to changes in their routines.

Preschoolers: three to five years old. The preschool years pose their own challenges. These children are too big to be carried, too big for strollers, and yet not quite strong enough to carry their own gear. An accomplished preschool hiker could hike 5–10 miles in a day, with frequent breaks and a wealth of hearty snacks. However, most preschoolers should only be expected to do a max of 3 miles a day.

HOW MANY CHILDREN AND ADULTS ARE GOING?
Group size needs to be evaluated on three levels:
1. How many children are going?
2. How old are they?
3. How many adults are going?

There are no magic numbers. It really depends on each group. Picture two couples going out, each with a young baby, all staying in the same cabin. It could be fabulous, or it could mean a lot of crying all night with one baby waking the other. Two toddlers will require much supervision around camp, but when traveling with a toddler and an older child, the older child will be more independent.

How much extra weight are the adults willing to carry? It is great to have at least one extra adult who doesn't have a child on the trip. This person can help hold babies, haul gear, and provide an extra set of eyes and hands. More hands are helpful, but make sure everyone going on the trip knows the limitations of traveling with a baby in tow and are cool with it.

HOW LONG WILL YOUR TRIP LAST?
How far are you going? Be realistic. Don't push it. Many injuries happen when people overestimate their abilities. Remember, your baby needs you to get him or her back home safely.

When you are just starting out, plan short hikes close to home. Then work up to an overnight trip. This allows you to work out some kinks and discover what your limits really are.

WHAT TIME OF YEAR IS IT?
Spring, summer, or fall on the same trail will yield three different hikes. Don't assume you know the trail if you haven't traveled it in the season you're planning your trip for. A trail that is usually pretty dry in the summer can be a creek walk in the spring. Another trail may be a beautiful summer hike but have high avalanche danger in the spring. And yet another trail in early June can be a nice, easy hike, but late in the summer the grass could have grown so tall and thick you can't even see the trail.

WHAT KIND OF GEAR DO YOU HAVE?

Never is there a better time to have a quality tent than when camping with little kids. Staying warm and dry at night isn't just a nice perk, it is a safety necessity. Proper sleeping bags and clothing become matters of survival in many climates.

TIPS & TRICKS

Outdoor gear stores often rent gear such as packs, tents, and personal flotation devices. This is especially helpful when you are planning a trip far from home or when you aren't ready to commit to buying your own gear. If you rent a tent, set it up at home to make sure that you know how and that no parts are missing.

Good gear makes all the difference in the wilderness. These tents all have ample guy lines and sturdy poles to withstand strong winds. [JEN AIST]

WHAT WILDLIFE OR PLANTS ARE YOU LIKELY TO ENCOUNTER?

Are the salmon running? Then you need to think about bear encounters. Is it swampy terrain? Then plan on a lot more bugs. Contact local authorities about likely wildlife in the area.

Check out some books on local flora and fauna for invaluable information. Familiarize yourself with native plants. Can you identify poison oak and ivy? Do you know which berries are edible? Find out before you go.

DO YOU HAVE A CONTINGENCY PLAN?

If you're planning a base-camping trip on an island in Prince William Sound, Alaska, do you have an alternate plan in case it rains cats and dogs the whole time? What will you do if it is just too hot to complete your hike to the bottom of the Grand Canyon in Arizona?

A contingency plan for rain might include choosing a large tent in case you need to spend the whole day in it. A hot-weather contingency plan might involve a shorter alternate route or a place to camp earlier than your planned destination. You may need to extend your trip, depending on these "on-the-trail" decisions, so make sure that folks back home are aware of possible alternate plans.

DAY HIKING

"The mountains are calling and I must go."
——John Muir, in a letter to his sister from Yosemite

Day hiking is one of my favorite activities. You can be spontaneous. You can try out a different trail every week. And if you're lucky, you can slow down and rediscover what young children find so fascinating about the smallest of things.

Newborns can be taken hiking as soon as their parents feel up to it. Newborns maintain their body temperature more consistently when you carry them. In one fascinating study of thermoregulation, the researcher put twins on their mom's chest, skin to skin. One baby was a little bit cool, and the other was a bit hot. Mom's chest naturally cooled the "hot" baby on the right while it warmed the "cool" one on the left. This happened at the same time. Our bodies are simply amazing. So plan on wearing your newborn rather than pushing him or her in a stroller.

New moms also need to remember that relaxin, the hormone that relaxes a woman's joints in anticipation of birth, is in her body for approximately three months after birth. Therefore, she needs to be careful while exercising to avoid injury. Consult your midwife or obstetrician before doing any strenuous hiking during the first two months postpartum.

On your first hike with your newborn, keep it simple and short. A two-hour walk is probably more than plenty. Julia, a longtime childbirth educator and lactation consultant, advises new moms to walk a bit one way from the car, then turn around and walk the same distance in the opposite direction. By doing this, you avoid walking too far away from the car, getting exhausted, and having to struggle on a long trip back to the car. This is especially important if mom is recovering from a cesarean birth. Be gentle!

PLANNING YOUR HIKE

It's true that day hikes can be spontaneous and relatively low-maintenance, but there are still many factors to consider when choosing a trail (see the following chart).

PACKING YOUR GEAR

Any parent will tell you that it takes twice as long to get out of the house once you have a baby. This is because it takes so long to pack. You are more likely to get out hiking more often if you keep a day pack gear-ready.

Smaller day packs: (Up to 1,525 cubic inches of capacity) Some specialized day packs include those for mountain marathons, which are of lighter construction and have external compression systems to keep your gear from bouncing around; they are designed to be stable on your back when you're running.

Larger day packs: (1,525–1,830 cubic inches of capacity) Look for any special features that you know you will need, such as ice ax loops or crampon straps if you are going snow hiking or side or lid pockets for easy access to photography equipment.

I have a summer hiking pack and a cool-season hiking pack for spring and

A small day pack and a baby carrier are all you need to take your baby for an afternoon walk. [AMELIA OLIVER]

Allow time to discover the little things on the trail. [JEN AIST]

PLANNING QUESTIONS	TRAIL CONSIDERATIONS
What is your goal for the trip?	Always make sure everyone on the hike—children included—is aware of the trip's goal. This will go far in keeping everyone satisfied.
	If the goal Is to cover some good distance and you are traveling with a preschooler, choose a trail from which you can see the destination. It's easier to hike uphill when you can see the top of the mountain than it is through a thick forest of trees.
	If the goal is a nature hike, choose a trail with a variety of ecosystems to provide ample opportunities for discovery.
What will your mode of travel be?	Research the width and smoothness of the trail if you'll be using a jogging stroller.
	If you are packing your child, you aren't limited by the width of the trail or the grade. I do not recommend river or stream crossings when carrying young children. Even knee-deep water can carry a current strong enough to knock over an adult. Don't take the chance. Choose another trail.
How old is your child?	**Infants** have little say in where they go. A hike with a young baby can easily be a workout hike for the parents or a gentle stroll, depending on your mood. Hike often when your baby is young. It really is the easiest time to do it.
	Toddlers are likely to hike at a slower pace. This is as it should be, since it is difficult to appreciate rocks and ladybugs at a brisk pace. For toddlers who will walk on their own, choose a nice, wide trail away from steep cliffs, so they have the freedom to run and explore on the trail. A trail with little elevation gain is a good idea too. Steep trails wear out small legs pretty fast. Choose trails for toddlers that will provide some fun opportunities for discovery along the way, such as a boardwalk with a fish-viewing platform, a trail with a beaver dam that is close enough to check out, or a path where butterflies like to hang out. Remember to bring a child carrier along for when your toddler needs a rest from hiking. Keep the hike's distance short so everyone has a good experience.
	Preschoolers can often hike a lot farther than you would expect. My oldest could easily do 10 miles in a day by age four. When my other three children were four years old, they maxed out at 5 miles. Learn your child's capacity. The average preschooler does just fine with 3- to 5-mile hikes. Preschoolers like trails with predictable milestones along the way, such as a notable bench; this can give young children a perspective of how far they have gone and how far they have to go. After all, 1, 5, or 10 miles has little meaning for young children. We have a favorite day hike on which, about a mile into it, there's a great hand tram across a gorge. Everyone is always excited to get to the tram. Looping back on the same trail allows the children to gauge how much farther it is to the car.

PLANNING QUESTIONS	TRAIL CONSIDERATIONS
How many children and adults are going?	Groups with numerous kids of varying ages need a trail that accommodates everyone (see the preceding question).
	Be mindful of the impact of a large group on the trail. Beyond their many footprints, large groups are also louder and generally more disruptive of nature. If you have several adults along, consider breaking up into smaller groups.
What time of year is it? What wildlife or plants are you likely to encounter?	Trails can change widely from one season to the next. Rain, ice, snow, or sun can transform an innocuous trail into a treacherous one.
	In hot or humid weather, look for trails that follow creeks or rivers, which will provide a way to cool off and a source of drinking water (once purified). Trails with shade trees or other sources of shade are great too.
	Spring hikes require a greater knowledge of the trail. Thin crusts of snow common in the spring can thinly veil creeks and other water sources.
	Consider what type of wildlife might be present. Spring is calving time; late summer to early fall is mating season. These are times when wildlife is best left alone.

fall. I keep everything I'm going to need for a day hike in each one. All I have to add is some food and water bottles, and we are on our way. While the specific items in your bag will vary depending on where you are hiking, the Ten Essentials are a good place to start (see also Checklists).

The Ten Essentials

1. **Map and compass.** We like to mark the spot on the map where we find different animals. This gives all us practice using a map and is fun to go back and review later. Another favorite activity is to name or rename peaks on the map.
2. **Sunglasses and sunscreen** (see the Sun chapter for details).
3. **Extra clothing.** I always leave an extra pair of kid socks in my pack. I also bring an extra layer in case the weather turns. I've never regretted carrying extra jackets.
4. **Headlamp or flashlight.** Even on a day hike, be prepared in case an emergency keeps you out after dark.
5. **First-aid kit.** Pack a lot of adhesive bandages. The power of 2 inches of adhesive never ceases to amaze me.
6. **Firestarter and cigarette lighter, flint stick, or matches.** These other "just-in-case" items are easy to pack.
7. **Knife.** Whether you use it for emergency repairs or just cutting up an apple at snacktime, it's a good tool to bring along.

8. **Extra snacks.** Pack some high-calorie bars the kids will eat. There is no point in bringing it if it tastes terrible and no one will eat it.

9. **Water bottles.** How much water you take along depends greatly on the climate. In a temperate climate, I bring one quart for myself and a pint for each child. These volumes should easily be tripled in hot or humid areas. If you are hiking in hot areas near water sources, bring along a water filter or purifier as well.

10. **Space blanket or emergency blanket.** This is on the "just-in-case" list. They don't take up much room and are superlight. Hopefully you will never need it, but in case you do get stuck somewhere, it can be a lifesaver.

Small packs carry water as well as treasured rocks and other important things for kids.
[JONATHAN DITTO]

In addition, depending on where you're hiking, the following items can come in very handy:
- insect repellent, head nets, anti-itch cream
- bear bells
- signaling device (Cell phones are great, but you can't guarantee coverage or battery life. Spots—satellite locator devices—are increasingly popular, but don't forget good old-fashioned mirrors and whistles, or smoke signaling techniques.)

Many new parents want to bring every possible piece of baby gear they might possibly need, everywhere they go. Here's the essential list for a day hike: two diapers and a few wipes. I promise you'll be OK for a couple of hours without the nail clippers, diaper creams, colic drops, and four changes of clothing. And trust me, you will be happier hiking without all the weight.

Junior Naturalist Options

Bring along some extra items, depending on your destination, that will keep your little ones happy exploring. Here are some items to consider:

- binoculars (Look for inexpensive ones for your budding naturalist to carry.)
- camera with extra batteries
- journal or notepad and colored pencils to take notes along the way (I love the Write in the Rain books; they are sturdy and hold up to wet environments.)
- bug net to catch and release butterflies
- field guides (Play around with identifying plants and animals.)

KEEPING THE HIKE FUN AND SAFE

If there is just one adult on the hike, he or she should walk behind the kids. This way, the adult can keep an eye on everyone, and each child gets a chance to be the leader. Rotate leaders throughout the hike so everyone who wants to can have a turn.

An adult's coat makes a simple nest for a napping newborn. [KARIN BRAUN]

Many families like to sing on the trail. See Resources for tips on how to find classic camping and hiking songs.

Plan for a lot of rest stops along the way. Everyone should take a drink and have a quick snack at each break. The trick is to have many short ones instead of a couple long ones. Five to ten minutes is usually plenty. The Washington Trails Association suggests announcing upcoming breaks by saying something like, "When we get to the big tree ahead, we'll need an energy break." This helps new hikers pace themselves.

If this is going to be a power hike, remind children at the trailhead. Don't take breaks in the beginning of a power hike, or you'll never get there. Tell the group you will break after passing twenty trees, thirty cacti, or some other tangible landmark. Celebrate each milestone with a treat such as a sticker for superhikers or a fruit snack.

Keep it positive. The goal is for everyone to have a good time and want to come out again. Tell your kids what fun it is to hike as a family. Show your children how much you genuinely enjoy being outside, and they will naturally want to follow suit. Experience the joy of being in nature with your children—what an incredible legacy that is to give them.

Day hikes are free, fun, and fabulous. Set a goal to do one a week.

CAR CAMPING

"Some national parks have long waiting lists for camping reservations. When you have to wait a year to sleep next to a tree, something is wrong."

—George Carlin

The United States is home to at least 8,000 public campgrounds and another 8,000 that are privately owned. That gives you plenty of options. Great resources to help you find and reserve campgrounds are available—both in print and on the Internet. Reserve America is probably the best first stop; you won't find every campground through this organization, but you will certainly have a good start.

CHOOSING THE PERFECT CAMPGROUND

Even with 16,000 campgrounds across fifty states, your choices may be limited. Some parts of the country have several campgrounds within a dozen miles of each other, while other areas have only one. When you have selected the part of the country you are going to visit, consider the following points if there is a choice among campgrounds in that area:

- **Size.** Campgrounds can be as small as a half dozen sites or as large as more than

400 sites in campgrounds like those at Yellowstone National Park. Some families prefer larger campgrounds with more amenities and increased opportunities for socializing with other campers. Others prefer more solitude.

- **Amenities.** If hot showers are important to you or your little ones, it may be worth it to drive a bit farther to a campground that has one. Similarly, a coin-operated laundry on-site can be important on longer trips.
- **Attractions.** Other things to look for include guided nature walks or presentations, trail systems attached to the campground, and perhaps a visitor center nearby with exhibits and short films.
- **Pavement.** Gravel roads are not ideal for little kids to bike on, and cars driving on them generate a lot of dust, so paved or unpaved roads are something to consider.
- **RV hookups.** Water and electrical hookups and sewage dump-out facilities are important to check for if you have a motor home, trailer, or pop-up. If you're tent camping, bear boxes for safely storing your food and/or bear-proof garbage containers are good things to check for.
- **Motorized vehicle and/or boat policies.** My family prefers hiking and boating in areas where motorized equipment is not allowed. I don't want a big roar disrupting our solitude while we're paddling along a lake. Likewise, a four-wheeler tearing down a trail is a real bummer. Imagine sitting quietly in a field having a snack when one of those flies by. This is a personal preference.

CHOOSING A CAMPSITE

Once you have chosen a campground, you need to choose a campsite. You might have few or many options here. Some campgrounds allow you to reserve a spot ahead of time, while others are first come, first served. Popular campgrounds might be full by noon or earlier, so try to arrive as early as possible if you don't have a reservation.

TIPS & TRICKS

To take some of the guesswork out of reserving a campsite at a campground you've never visited, try to look at a map of the campground online. The sites are usually numbered, the campground's road system shows site locations, and you can look for amenities such as restrooms and play areas.

Sarah from Michigan has perfected her site selection technique. First she drives around the whole loop, scoping out all the bathrooms and water pumps. She likes to be near a bathroom but not next to it. Her children are three and five, so when they need to use the potty, they need to go immediately. But her family doesn't want to listen to everyone else using the toilet all night either. Sarah's family doesn't need to collect water that often, so proximity to the water pump isn't crucial.

Then she investigates which campsites seem to be the noisiest in terms of traffic and socializing. If radios are already blaring at ten in the morning, she crosses that section off her list.

They usually pull a trailer with all of their camping gear in it, and while Sarah's

This is one well-organized camp; notice the bins under the table to organize kitchen gear, as well as the water station on the right-hand table. [MICHAEL ELDRIDGE]

husband is great at backing it in, Sarah admits she's terrible at it. So she prefers a site with a loop driveway that she can just pull the van through.

A final tip Sarah shared is this: when her family finds a site they really love, they write down its number to remember it for their next trip.

Setting Up Camp

The more efficiently you can set up your campsite, the more time you'll have to play. Organization starts in your sleeping area, so set up the tent first (see the Sleep chapter for basics such as tent sites and sleep gear).

The Sleeping Area

It is so much easier to keep kids warm and dry when you can easily find gear when you need it rather than rifling through all the bags every time. Duct tape and a marker pen are great labeling tools. Organize kids' clothes by layer: a bag for outerwear, insulating layers, swimwear, sleepwear, maybe even one bag just for socks.

Bring along a duffle bag or a laundry basket for all dirty clothes. Children—even one-year-olds—can be taught to put their dirty clothes in the right spot. The younger you give children the skills needed to help out around camp, the better.

The Kitchen

Most campgrounds include a fire ring and a picnic table. Some campgrounds also have grill stands; others have nothing at all. Regardless of the existing amenities, here are some key items to bring along:

Washing dishes is a breeze in a small collapsible sink. [JEN AIST]

Portable camping table: This incredibly useful item can be used for food prep, as a table for appetizers, or even as a washup station. Folding camp tables, which are usually made of vinyl or metal, can be cleaned more thoroughly than wooden tables, too. Many families bring a vinyl tablecloth to put over the picnic table for easier cleaning.

Clamp-on baby chair or booster seat: Many clamp-on chairs fit on picnic tables, allowing your baby to sit at the table with the family. Some tables are too thick for these seats, though, in which case a booster seat can be strapped to the table's bench for the baby. If all else fails, your lap always works just fine.

Artificial turf: Kristen from Arizona always brings a piece of rolled-up artificial turf to place in the kitchen area. She says less dust is stirred up around the table, keeping dirt out of the food she is preparing, and it doubles as a play mat for her eight-month-old son.

Cleaning supplies: Set up a bucket, a collapsible sink, or a plastic washtub for washing dishes, with a small bottle of biodegradable dish soap and some sponges nearby. After a meal, all leftover scraps can go in a trash bag and the dishes go in the bucket. Be sure to follow local guidelines regarding disposal of wastewater and garbage.

Food bins: Much of the day can revolve around mealtimes, so do your best to organize your food. Use coolers, bins, and/or car-camping organizers. Plan a secure spot to store your food when you're away from camp; if bear-proof lockers are provided, use them. Help do your part to keep wild animals wild.

Play Areas—Theirs and Yours

As a hardcore believer in open-ended play, I find it is important to organize toys and equipment for children, although this might sound contradictory. When you make items such as magnifying glasses, bug nets, journaling materials, and buckets readily available, kids are much more likely to use them. Having a clearly defined storage space makes keeping track of these items a breeze.

To encourage creative play, I advocate organizing the gear, not the play. It's like setting out a bird feeder. You fill it up with enticing seeds, then walk away and find a quiet spot to watch the magic of your children connecting to nature—truly a treat!

If your family prefers to stay at the campground all day, try laying out different items to play with throughout the day. For example, put out a bin of sidewalk chalk in the morning. After a while, your kids will tire of this activity. Put it away and get out some flying discs or balls to throw. If you have too many options out at one time, the kids will get overwhelmed and not play productively with any of it, so switch out items frequently. (This trick works magic at home as well.)

Balancing kid time and adult time is always important—at home and at camp. Establishing camping routines and sticking to them is one way to make sure the adults get some down time. (For more on routines, see the Sleep chapter.) Consider setting up a baby monitor when the kids go to bed. That way, when the adults are sitting around the campfire, they can easily keep track of the kids sleeping in the tent or the camper.

BASE CAMPING

"But the place which you have selected for your camp, though never so rough and grim, begins at once to have its attractions, and becomes a very centre of civilization to you: 'home is home, be it never so homely.'"

—Henry David Thoreau, *The Maine Woods*

Base camping has many variations, but a popular version with children involves the family getting dropped off at a given location, then taking shorter day trips from there. Base camping is similar to car camping in some ways but also decidedly different, because it involves getting off the road system and into remote areas. Base camping is a great option for folks wanting to have a remote wilderness experience without a whole lot of physical work getting there. It is also ideal for groups of children of various ages.

After our twins were born, my husband and I struggled to find ways to take our four children under the age of five out into the backcountry. Backpacking was out because the two of us really couldn't carry gear for all six of us on our backs. The babies were too young for a biking trip, and a drive-to campground wasn't always "wild" enough for us.

Luckily, we were in the same boat as a couple of other families. We put our heads and our money together and chartered a boat to drop us off on a remote beach along Alaska's Prince William Sound. Four families and eleven children under the age of five set up camp under the midnight sun in the shadows of a glacier. Breakfast was a communal affair, with the oldest kids taking responsibility for blueberry picking. If you haven't had hot pancakes made with freshly picked blueberries, you are missing out! For lunch every family was on their own, and each family chose a night to cook dinner.

We brought a half dozen kayaks and took turns paddling around the bay. There were always at least two adults on the beach to watch however many kids stayed on-shore. Each couple had time to go out and paddle each day. The beachgoers went on day hikes around the island, scavenged for rocks, played hide-and-go-seek, and basically relaxed. A dozen or so trips later, we have polished our strategies for site selection, menu planning, and the "what to do if it rains horizontally for the whole week" contingency plan.

SAFETY TIP

If you are being dropped off by small plane or motorboat, provide some ear protection for your baby. Some parents use dog earmuffs, which are triangular and have a hook-and-loop-fastened strap. Baby Banz makes earmuffs specifically for babies that are reasonably priced and fit little heads well.

CHOOSING THE PERFECT SITE

Site selection is the most critical decision in designing a successful base-camping trip. Beaches on oceans, lakes, and rivers are common, but other options certainly exist. You can be dropped off by plane, boat, or pack animals. Study a map carefully and ask yourself the following questions to decide where to go.

What activities does the location allow? Many great camping beaches can be found along coastlines, but many are set at the bottom of steep cliffs, bordered by impassable rocks, or subject to extreme tides that shrink the beach size twice a day, which isolates you to a much smaller section of beach. Look for a spot that allows for some hiking and exploring as well. Is fishing allowed? Boating? Rock climbing? Fossil searching? Gold mining? Berry picking?

Is the site large enough to support your group? You need enough space to set up all your tents and a kitchen area. You also need enough space that you aren't making a big impact on the area. You need space to spread out.

Is there any natural shelter? Trees provide great shade and offer

WILD FACT
Pack Stock

Pack animals have served folks heading into the backcountry forever. Horses, donkeys, mules, llamas, and more have hauled our gear and ourselves into remote areas for extended trips that would otherwise not be possible.

some protection from rainy weather. Rock outcroppings protect from wind. A point mutes the waves a bit.

PLANNING YOUR ADVENTURE

If you are camping with more than one family, consider having a limited amount of structure around your day. For example, it is easier to cook breakfast once for the whole group rather than multiple times. I can't encourage you enough to have a pretrip meeting with every family who is going on the trip. At this meeting, you need to discuss the questions listed in the Trip Planning chapter.

If everyone is on the same page, base camping with friends and family is a great adventure. You'll want to plan a trip every summer.

TIPS & TRICKS

Put two camping chairs together front to front for a nice little cot for a napping child.

Nature provides the simplest and best toys. [TOM TWIGG]

PACKING YOUR GEAR

Depending on how you'll be dropped off, you can bring along some nice luxury items if space and weight limits allow.

Screen tent: Seriously consider bringing a screen tent, which comes in many sizes and styles. They provide some shade, are sturdy, and have screening that goes all the way down, all the way around. This tent provides respite from bugs and sun and is a great napping area for young children. Mike and Helena set theirs up next to their sleeping tent and use it as a dressing room; the extra room is very helpful for getting everyone dressed.

Portable folding tables: If space allows, bring at least two folding tables for the kitchen. They make food prep and cooking much easier.

Camping chairs: Sometimes sitting off the ground is a good thing. Camp chairs fold up easily for transport and can be quickly stashed if it rains.

Coolers: If you can bring a cooler, and bears aren't an issue where you're going, bring it. Coolers allow for a much wider menu selection, but their size and weight often prohibit bringing them. When we camp near glaciers, we have an unlimited supply of ice to keep our coolers cold. There's nothing like hauling million-year-old ice out of the ocean to keep your drinks cold!

Once you know what gear you'll be bringing, how you pack it will make a big impact on the enjoyment of your trip. Spend the extra time at home to make sure you have everything very organized. Kendra, who co-wrote the Food chapter, uses duct tape to label bags and bins, and *everything* is labeled. One food

It takes a lot of gear to outfit four families for one week at a base camp. [JEN AIST]

bin says "snacks," another "lunch." She also labels a bag for guidebooks and colored pencils. Her kids' clothes are organized by layer, and sometimes she even puts a colored dot on the bags so the kids can find their own gear. She'll say, "Your socks are in the blue dot bag," so the child can go get them. Though she spends a considerable amount of time organizing before a base-camping trip, she swears it's always worth it.

SETTING UP CAMP

When you arrive at your site with all your gear in a big mound, it's time to set up camp. Sorting through multiple families' gear can be a chore, but if you bring some hardy kids along, they like to help and want important jobs around camp. Don't be shy about giving out jobs. Even little two-year-olds can help carry gear from the drop site to the

A base camp for twenty people on a one-week trip looks like a small village. [JEN AIST]

campsite. Preschoolers love to be the ones to clear out rocks and sticks at the tent site. And when children are occupied, they are less likely to be injured.

The Tents

Set up your tents well away from the kitchen area. Concentrating your cooking, eating, and sleeping areas into one spot increases your impact on the area. It can also bring critters that are attracted to your kitchen too close to your sleeping area. Look for a flat area away from possible water runoff. Take your time to find the best tent locations. If the weather isn't cooperating on the first day, set up your tents quickly and scout out a better location when conditions allow.

The Kitchen

Set up a well-organized kitchen area well away from water sources. I use one portable camping table for a double-burner camp stove and another for food prep, such as chopping and stirring. Weather conditions and local wildlife will determine the best way to secure your food. Eat sitting on camp chairs or on the ground; usually space doesn't allow enough portable tables to sit at for meals.

The Toilet Area

You can let each person dig a new cat hole for each potty run, or you can set up a group potty area. To further lessen your impact and your digging time, consider bringing a potty you can pack out. A family of four out for one week will produce quite a bit of poop. That's a pretty big footprint to leave behind for the next users, but imagine the impact of a group of twenty folks. Situate the toilet area well away from the tent and kitchen areas. See the Dirt chapter for more on group potties.

BACKPACKING

With contributions from Jane Hodgson

"Backpacking is the art of knowing what not to take."
— Sheridan Anderson, *Baron Von Mabel's Backpacking*

Pregnant moms and dads are always telling me how sad they are to put their backpacks to rest for the next ten years after the baby is born. I am here to tell you that you don't have to do that! Babies make the best backpacking partners, but you can backpack with children of any age.

My first backpacking trip with my oldest daughter, when she was an infant, was a rite of passage for me. I wasn't totally convinced it would work out well, but I knew if it did, I could do anything as a mom. I figured out that I had everything I needed right on my back to take care of myself and my infant daughter. I found backpacking with my baby to be liberating and empowering. The sky was the limit—I could go anywhere.

Today, this same child absolutely loves hiking. By age ten she was carrying a 20-pound backpack on 40-mile trips. Now at age twelve, she and I plan to hike the Chilkoot Trail, made famous during Alaska's 1896 gold rush. My daughter frequently writes in school papers about her experiences in the woods. I can tell by her words that these trips have been equally empowering for her as a young lady. So take my advice and hit the trail with your children early and often.

CHOOSING A BACKPACK

Most people who are regularly in the outdoors have a selection of backpacks to choose from, depending on the length and nature of the trip and the season. Look for a backpack with an adjustable back system, broad and well-padded hip and shoulder straps, and a chest (sternum) strap.

What Size Do You Need?

Decide what size backpack you need. A backpack that is too big tends to get overfilled, and you end up carrying more weight than you need. If you carry one that's too small, you might have a problem on colder days when you need more gear and either end up underequipped or having equipment hanging off the pack, which can unbalance it. Generally, backpacks are measured in liters of capacity, or volume.

Small multiday backpacks: (2,135–3,355 cubic inches of capacity) Useful for single overnight trips in hostels or huts, these also can be larger climbing or mountaineering packs.

Large multiday backpacks: (3,355-plus cubic inches of capacity) These allow you to carry the heaviest load, so it is absolutely imperative for the health of your spine to get the correct fit.

How Does It Fit?

A good backpack will last for years, so it is well worth getting one that fits you correctly.

Determine your back length. Backpacks either come in different back lengths or have an adjustable back system. To determine which size is correct for you, figure out your back length:

1. Find the most prominent knob at the base of your neck, just above the level of your shoulders (the C7 vertebra).
2. Find the iliac crests of your pelvis: stand with your hands on your waist, then slide your hands down until you find the top of your pelvis bones. Project a horizontal line from here inward to your spine.
3. Use a flexible tape measure to measure the distance between the two points. You'll need a friend to help you do this.

Consider gender-specific design. Don't forget that many backpacks are made in a male and a female fit. Female versions tend to allow for narrower shoulders, shorter back length, and wider hips. That doesn't mean that if you are a woman you must buy a female backpack. Women with long backs may get a better fit from a male backpack, whereas smaller-framed men with narrower shoulders should also try female backpacks for size.

Try it on. Go to a specialist retailer to try the backpack on. Find an outdoor retailer that has staff trained in fitting backpacks. To check the fit of a backpack:

1. Loosen all the straps.
2. If the pack has an adjustable back system, check that it is set to the correct length for you.

3. Tighten the hip belt snugly around the top of your pelvis, not around your stomach. It should be tight enough to transfer the load to your legs, so your shoulders aren't carrying the weight, but not so tight that it's uncomfortable.
4. Tighten the shoulder straps. Do not overtighten, or the hip belt will be lifted up.
5. Tension the load adjusters on the shoulder straps and the waist belt to stabilize the pack.
6. Fasten the chest (or sternum) strap. This can be uncomfortable, especially for women, if it is too low. The chest strap should be roughly level with the bottom of your armpits.

SAFETY TIP

With a good-quality, correctly fitted backpack, the hip belt will pass 80 percent of the load directly to your legs, thus avoiding stress on your shoulders and spine.

Keep pack sizes appropriate for the age of the child. [JEN AIST]

PACKING YOUR GEAR

There really is an art to deciding what goes in your backpack and what stays home. While some items are essential, most gear you think you need for your baby can easily be left behind. You'll also want to load your pack wisely and handle it carefully to protect your back.

Minimize the Weight You Carry

Every piece of camping gear needs to be scrutinized before it goes in your pack. Every ounce counts. Keep the weight down. Each item's weight is useful to know as you decide what to bring.

While there are no steadfast rules, a general guideline is to carry no more than about 25 percent to 30 percent of your body weight. This means a 140-pound person should limit the weight he or she is carrying to about 35 pounds, including the baby. Keep in mind that the 25 percent to 30 percent rule will change in some cases; the accompanying chart offers some handy parameters.

If you are hiking in hot climates, don't forget how much water you'll need to carry. Water weighs 8 pounds per gallon, so enough for a multiday trip can easily weigh 20 pounds.

There is no need to go out underequipped in bad weather, but critically examine what you are carrying and keep weight to a minimum. It is important to take good care of your back. Remember, you'll have to hike back out too.

HIKER	OPTIMAL BACKPACK WEIGHT
Pregnant mom	20 pounds max
Parent carrying an infant	35 pounds including the baby
Parent carrying gear	45 pounds
Toddler	1–2 pounds in a very small day pack
Preschooler	5 pounds max in a small day pack

Load It Carefully

Keep any heavy items at the bottom and close to your spine to reduce the strain on your back. Keep snacks, water bottles, and your camera in easy reach. I like to wear a fanny pack on my front for these items.

SAFETY TIP

Pack fuel toward the bottom of your pack and food near the top. If fuel leaks on your gear, it's not pleasant, but you can live with it and clean it up later. If the fuel leaks onto your food, you have to toss the food out.

Handle the Pack Safely

Before you think about carrying children on the trail, be sure you know the basics of carrying a backpack. (Although this information is written about a pack full of gear, the same principles apply to a pack with a child in it.) Protect your spine by using and handling your backpack correctly.

Practice picking it up and putting it down. The easiest way to damage your spine is to lift a heavy weight with your spine flexed and then to twist; yet this is how most of us pick up a loaded backpack. To put on a heavy pack without damaging your spine, either lift it up to about the height of your hips and place it on a surface or, if you are out with friends, help each other lift up your packs to the correct height. This way it's a straight lift rather than a lift and twist, and you are a lot less likely to hurt your spine.

PLANNING YOUR BACKPACKING TRIP

For your first trip, go out for just one night; then gradually add on more nights and miles. Despite all of your best planning and previous backpacking experience, you

Fun, short trips will get you ready for longer multiday trips with your baby. [LIZZY DONOVAN]

will need to work out kinks on the way. It is best to not do a test run that is a week long. When you're ready to do two nights, consider doing both nights in one campsite. Once you have had a couple of great short trips, you can start branching out into longer trips.

Backpacking While Pregnant

Moms can continue to backpack during pregnancy, but they do need to take some precautions, just as they do with any exercise regimen. The hormone that relaxes the joints in anticipation of birth also puts moms at risk for injury during weight-bearing exercise.

An expecting mom's growing belly will skew her center of gravity as well. Therefore, moms should limit the amount of weight they carry; 20 pounds is the maximum for most women. This is a great time to get into ultralight backpacking. Buckle the hip belt low, under your belly; it will help distribute the weight from the backpack as well as provide support to the joints of the pelvis.

This mom is ready to go with her baby on the front and a load on her back. [SUSAN GAULKE]

The current recommendation from the American College of Obstetricians and Gynecologists is to limit exercise in pregnancy to the extent that Mom can still talk easily while working out and she isn't overheated. This means a slower hike with more breaks. But the breaks will allow you time to appreciate the smaller joys of being in the backcountry, such as just sitting and listening to the forest.

Carrying Infants

Babies are positively the easiest children to backpack with. The younger, the better. They are totally content to be carried all day; they just drink milk; their gear is lightweight and easy to pack.

Try out your gear. Test out all of your gear ahead of time at home. Make sure you have a system to keep everyone warm and dry at night and not too hot in the day. Set up the tent in your yard, fill it with your sleeping bags and other gear, and make sure everyone will fit. Use test trips to the playground to make sure hats will stay on. Test out raingear and insulating layers on day hikes. Also go on a plethora of day hikes first to learn your and your baby's limits.

Plan your route. When you are planning your backpacking route, remember that you will need to stop for breaks more frequently with a baby in tow. If you usually plan 12- to 14-mile days without a baby, try 7- to 10-mile days with one. You are better off reaching camp feeling as though you could have gone farther, rather than feeling like you couldn't go another step. Remember you'll also need enough energy to set up camp, cook and eat dinner, and get everyone ready for bed.

When you're ready to do a longer trip, stay both nights in one campsite. This is especially important if your baby is sensitive to routines and environments. I always planned the length of backpacking trips by the number of dirty diapers I was willing to haul out. With the twins, the trips got shorter for diaper reasons alone.

Decide how to carry your baby and gear. As discussed in Part II, Transporting Little Ones on the Trail, you have options. One parent can carry the baby in a soft-sided carrier, sling, or wrap in front and carry the gear in a regular backpack on their back.

You can also use a jogging stroller or pack animals to carry the gear while you carry just the baby. Some families prefer to have one parent carry the baby and baby gear while the second parent carries all the camping gear.

Kimmer went backpacking with her first baby, Connor, when he was about ten months old. She packed him in an external-frame baby carrier while her partner, Aaron, carried almost everything else. Kimmer carried the baby's clothes and diapers—secure in the pocket of the baby carrier—but nothing else on her back. She also wore a fanny pack that held a first-aid kit, knife, compass, maps, and other odds and ends. If you have a hiking partner like Aaron who doesn't mind the extra weight, this is a good way to go.

Carrying twins while backpacking is a bit trickier. With very young twins, each parent could carry a baby in a front pack and a backpack of gear on back. With twins at least six months old, one person could carry a baby on the front and one on the back, while the other person carries all the gear. However, as babies get bigger, it gets more difficult to carry them on your front, especially when you are carrying a full pack on your back. With our twins, we usually ended up carrying one baby and pushing the other in a jogging stroller. Single strollers are much more trail-friendly than doubles.

Campsites that are accessible both by boat and trail open up a whole new option in gear hauling. One person can boat in all the gear while the other hikes in carrying just the baby. This is an especially good idea if you want to have a boat at camp but the conditions aren't safe for having a baby in the boat en route.

Toting Toddlers

Backpacking with toddlers is a completely different matter. This age group is often too heavy to carry yet not big enough to tote their own gear. Toddlers by nature are very attached to their routines, and backpacking has serious potential to disrupt these routines.

Plan your route. If you are doing a multiday trip, don't make the first day a long hike. Allow plenty of time for the unexpected. You don't want to have to push the group beyond their limits to get to camp by dark. Limit the hike to no more than 2–3 miles for toddlers hiking on their own. For children who will be pushed or pulled, limit the hike to about four to five hours max.

Decide how to transport your toddler and gear. The best way to take toddlers backpacking on any trip longer than about 3 miles is to push them in a jogging stroller. This limits the trails you can go on, but it also makes the trip a positive one for all involved.

Beth and her husband once took their young baby and toddler out on a family backpacking trip in the Ozarks on the Buffalo National River Area trails. She carried the baby in a Baby Bjorn and wore her backpack on her back. Her husband carried most of the gear, roughly 60 pounds, on his back. The plan was for their three-year-old to walk himself.

It wasn't a very strenuous trail, and their toddler had done a considerable amount of hiking, so they felt he could handle it, but he got tired and they didn't have time to keep stopping for breaks. It was getting dark and they really needed to get to their campsite. So Beth's husband ended up carrying the toddler too. Beth felt terrible.

The next day, the family set out earlier to allow for plenty of breaks, but Beth's husband still ended up carrying the toddler quite a bit. The next trip, the family borrowed a jogging stroller and used it for their toddler when he needed a break from hiking. It made all the difference. Though Beth said it was somewhat of a hassle to push an empty stroller at times, it was worth it—especially when their little boy was asleep.

If you plan on using a jogging stroller on your hike, make sure the whole trail is jogger friendly. Ask locals or local authorities about rocky trails, creek crossings, or narrow trails with steep drop-offs, all of which make using a jogging stroller difficult to impossible. National parks, state parks, Forest Service ranger stations, Bureau of Land Management offices, or any other agency can give you information. Be sure to ask specific questions; chances are, these rangers or guides have not hiked the trail with a jogging stroller in tow. Any trail marked "handicapped accessible" will work beautifully for a jogging stroller.

Toddlers usually really like to carry their own pack. Many companies make very small backpacks designed just for the youngest hikers. Kids from about eighteen months to three years old can easily carry their water bottle and a small snack.

Backpacking with Preschoolers

Preschool-aged children can carry a bit more but still not all of their gear. By age

Young backpackers sometimes need a hand on the trail. [JEN AIST]

five, most kids can carry their water bottle, snacks, and extra clothing layers. Their total pack weight, including the pack itself, should be less than 5 pounds. This means you will be carrying all of their gear.

Preschoolers are usually too big for jogging strollers, which means you lose their extra carrying capacity, so look extra closely at everything you are bringing. Every item in your pack should be able to take on more than one role.

Don't expect kids to carry all their own gear until about age eight or nine. At this age, youths can carry up to a maximum of 20 percent of their weight on their backs. Osprey and Mountainsmith both make great youth backpacks. The transition to carrying a full pack is a seamless one for kids who have been camping since they were babies.

BOATING

"Twenty years from now you will be more disappointed by the things that you didn't do than by the ones you did do. So throw off the bowlines. Sail away from the safe harbor. Catch the trade winds in your sails. Explore. Dream. Discover."

—Mark Twain

Bringing babies and young children out boating is a subject that could really be a book unto itself. This chapter is intended as an introduction or teaser to the wonderful world of boating with kids. Boating is such a great way to explore the coastline and inland waters with your children. From the water, you get a completely different perspective of land and (forgive me for growing a little philosophical) life as well. In many cases, you can explore coastline that is otherwise inaccessible. There is something incredibly humbling and at the same time empowering about cruising along in a boat powered by nothing but you and the water.

It's good to remember that children have been part of the backcountry forever. A friend of mine tells a story of kayaking in the Aleutians of Alaska, a string of remote islands in the Bering Sea. This friend was navigating the waters in a much smaller craft than a crab boat. He pulled up at a beach in his fiberglass boat and rubber boots, clad head to toe in the latest synthetic materials. An hour or so later, another boat joined him—a traditional kayak made of skins. An Aleut gentleman got out, pulled his boat up the beach a bit farther, and then poked his head into the cockpit and called out some names. Moments later, his wife and child climbed out of the bow, and together they set up camp. For eons, families have routinely boated, camped, hunted, and hiked all over the country. It wasn't always a special adventure; it was just life, and no one thought twice about it until very modern history.

When we first moved to Alaska, we met an incredible family who took their three children boating often. They even once floated the Yukon River with their six-month-old! When we met them, they took us out sea kayaking with their five-year-old son for a week. At the time, we didn't have children, and their ease of bringing their children into wild places was inspiring. In fact, it was that trip that convinced me to never stop adventuring, no matter how many kids we had.

LEARN WATER SAFETY SKILLS

That said, because we are land mammals that breathe air, being on the water does hold quite a few inherent risks for us. I am adamant about promoting safety and quality gear.

No one should go boating without experience. Sign up for classes, attend pool sessions, master skills on flat water, or hire a guide to take you. Boating with babies, toddlers, or preschoolers is worth the prep work.

Teach your children water safety, including how to swim. Most communities offer parent-baby swim classes beginning with infants at around six months of age. With regular practice and lessons, children can swim independently by age three or four. Children need to able to swim to the side of the pool and pull themselves out safely.

Before you head out on a boating trip, set up your boat on the lawn and practice where everyone will sit and everything will be stowed. Then practice paddling with a baby or toddler on your lap and make sure you can safely pilot your boat like that. If it won't work on your lawn, it certainly won't work on the water. Practicing at home gives you time to rearrange and get it right.

PFDS ARE YOUR BFF

Even families who spend months at a time on sailboats require their babies and young children to wear a personal flotation device (PFD) at all times on deck. I also recommend that children wear their PFD when they're on the shores of fast rivers. It doesn't take much to knock a small child into the water, and a good current will sweep him or her off all too quickly. I've heard too many tales of unsteady toddlers being knocked into rivers and lakes just by dogs running past. Children should always wear PFDs on docks as well, because they can easily fall in between boats or the dock and get seriously injured.

When children learn early on that taking off their PFD is not an option, they quickly get used to wearing it and stop fussing about it. They are also less apt to protest if the adults are wearing their vests as well. After the first hour or so, my kids forget they are even wearing it.

Choosing a PFD

PFDs will work only if they are in good condition and properly fitted. The U.S. Coast Guard recommends that you check your PFD often for any rips, tears, or holes. There should be *no* holes—not even small ones—and the seams, straps, and hardware should be in good condition. If the PFD is not in good shape, throw it away and get a new one. Never alter a PFD. If it is worn out, just get a new one.

Fitting a PFD

Personal flotation devices have come a long way since their debut on the *Titanic*. They are now lightweight and less bulky, and they come in all shapes and sizes. Many companies make infant-sized PFDs. Here's how to fit your child's PFD:

- Put the vest on your child and buckle it up.
- Pick up your child by the shoulders of the vest. The top of the vest's shoulders should not reach up past your child's chin and ears.
- If they do, try tightening the buckles.
- If that doesn't work, pick a smaller vest.

Having a PFD that fits well and is comfortable makes boating with infants as small as 9 pounds a reality. [JUNIPER MACFARLANE]

Test out your PFD on your child in a swimming pool before you go boating. Different body shapes and sizes float differently in different PFDs. You want the PFD to support your baby or child when they're on their back with their head well supported.

You may have to try more than one style to find one that works well for your child. Choose your child's PFD well, because your baby will be wearing it full-time on the water.

KID OVERBOARD!

If for any reason your child ever falls in the water (whether off a dock, out of a boat, or at the shore of a fast river), try to grab the handle of the PFD and haul your child back in.

Make sure your child is still breathing, then get him or her into dry clothes and warmed up. You may need to go to shore to properly warm up your child, depending on the weather. An infant will warm more quickly if placed skin to skin with an adult. These are the specific guidelines for warming a person who has been submerged in cold water:

- Remove the victim from the cold.
- Get the person dry and keep him or her dry.
- Insulate the person from the ground and get him or her to eat and move his or her body.
- Reinsulate with dry insulation.
- Cover and protect the head from further heat loss.
- Cover and protect the hands and feet from frostbite.
- Surround with a windproof and waterproof layer.
- If conscious, feed warm, sweet liquids.
- If unconscious, evacuate and handle very gently.

SAFETY TIP

Down sleeping bags and down clothing are not appropriate water-sports gear. Stick with materials that will keep their loft when wet and dry easily when the sun returns, such as fleece and synthetic fill.

PLANNING A BOATING TRIP

Tips and tricks for successful boating adventures vary depending on the body of water you'll be visiting and the type of boating you'll be doing. Make sure you research the body of water from quality guidebooks, from locals who know the area, and from area land managers. There are no exceptions to doing this research. Scope the map closely for campsites and emergency pullouts. On your trip, check these spots out and make notes on your map for future trips.

Remember that unlike hiking, when the child is walking and carrying a small pack, young children don't have as much to do on the boat. Planning some activities to keep them busy and entertained on the water is key. The following sections on four popular types of boating adventures offer tips for family outings with children from infants to toddlers and preschoolers.

SAILING

As is true with all boating, you need one adult dedicated to caring for the children and another adult to pilot the boat. The pilot should be able to pilot the boat solo if necessary.

Sailing with Infants

You have two main challenges when sailing with infants: keeping them safe from weather exposure and keeping them safe from going overboard. For the first challenge, see the Sun chapter and "Water Sports" in the Clothing chapter.

Safety. For the second challenge, even with an adult dedicated to holding the baby, there will be times when that adult will need to put the baby down. There are many different methods of securing the baby in those instances.

A hammock is probably the easiest to set up in the cabin, and it will cradle the baby in a nice nest. Lightweight models are made of nylon or mesh and have S hooks or carabiners to attach to anchor points on the boat.

Another option is to strap an infant car seat to something in the cockpit or cabin. The baby can then sit in the seat while wearing a PFD. It is not recommended to strap the baby into the car seat in this scenario. If the car seat were to break loose and go into the water, the baby's PFD would not function properly.

Jennifer has sailed often with her two children, ever since they were babies. She secured a booster seat with a tray (the kind you would use at the dinner table) to a seat in the cockpit. This way the baby could sit securely and doodle or snack on the tray while mom and dad tended to the sails.

In the cabin, the baby does not need to wear a PFD all the time. However, on deck the baby must always wear a PFD, even if you are carrying the baby in a sling or a soft-structured baby carrier.

Diapers. Most families advise using disposable diapers on sailboats because space is always at a premium on boats, and freshwater can be scarce if you're not sailing on a lake. Consider bringing a five-gallon bucket that can be locked closed to contain the dirties and allow for easier dumping onshore.

Sleep. Babies tend to sleep well on boats due to the constant rocking motion and, surprisingly, don't get motion sick very often. Babies can sleep in the berths, in portable playpens, on nests made of clothing on the floor, in hammocks, or with parents. You can close in a V berth by attaching fishnet along the open end on stretch cord. The netting can be pulled aside like a curtain when not in use.

Sailing with Toddlers

Toddlers can go sailing, too, but they are generally harder to manage on a boat. They are busy, fast, and unsteady, which can be a really bad combination. But some key tricks can make sailing with this age group go smoothly.

Safety. It is imperative to have an adult assigned to kid patrol. The ratio should be one adult for each toddler. Just as with any other type of camping, try to have some sense of routine for your toddler while sailing. Use fishnet to close off the gap along the lifelines of the boat.

Motion sickness. Toddlers (and older children) can get motion sickness, even if they have been sailing since birth. Frequently offer snacks with protein to help calm the tummy. Cheese or trail mix with a lot of seeds can do wonders. While many recommend ginger ale and saltines for a queasy stomach, the high amount of carbohydrates in these snacks usually makes matters worse. Sea bands (elastic cuffs with small plastic studs that activate acupressure points in the wrist) work with some kids, too.

Play. Keep 'em busy! Consider activities such as watching for dolphins or "painting" the boat with water and a paintbrush. Get creative and have fun. And when you are feeling exhausted at the end of watching them all day, remember that while toddlers require a lot of energy to keep up with, they really are at an exciting age, full of discovery and wonder.

Sailing with Preschoolers

By preschool age, kids who have grown up around boats are increasingly independent but still not ready to be turned

Fishnet (here, placed below the bowsprit) protects children from falling off a sailboat.
[HEIDI BARKER]

loose. PFDs are still mandatory on deck, and slopping on sunscreen is still a daily ritual. Preschoolers are steadier on their feet and a bit less impulsive than toddlers, but they still require frequent supervision, and routines are still important.

Safety. Attach fishnet to the lifelines to help prevent slips into the water. Follow my friend Jennifer's rule for her children: "One hand on the boat and one hand for you." This means the children are not allowed to carry anything when walking around on the boat. One hand is available to grab onto something solid onboard, and the other is available for bracing themselves. When the seas are rough, young children should stay in the cabin.

SEA KAYAKING

Full-fledged sea kayaking trips might be better postponed until your children are school age, but base camping allows you to go out for a paddle with younger children on calm days; you can stay back at camp with unfavorable weather. While it may be tempting, do not ever put a child in a kayak's gear hatch. Gear hatches are important to the flotation of your sea kayak when it is overturned or taking on water.

This future captain enjoys her sailing time on deck. [TOM TWIGG]

Sea Kayaking with Infants

Kayaking with babies works in some environments, but not in others. Extended trips in cold water are difficult at best with babies. If you have to paddle in varied weather conditions, you are at risk for going into the water. Paddling with a baby on your lap diminishes your ability to brace the kayak in rough water. You'll also want your spray skirt on in rougher water, which doesn't work with a baby on your lap. This doesn't mean you can't take a baby out—just that you need ideal conditions for it.

Safety. Young infants need to have their PFD on and either be worn in some quick-drying soft baby carrier or be positioned between your knees.

My youngest daughter loved going out in the sea kayak. When she was about six months old, we would take her out for an hour or two at a time in a bay. I had her sit between my knees, between myself and the paddle, on a folding backpacking chair. Her PFD, especially the headrest, increased her girth to a point that it made it difficult for me to efficiently paddle the kayak. I had to extend my arms out quite a bit to get around her. If I had had to travel any distance, I would have had a difficult time. But for toodling around in the bay, it was great.

Dad and daughter enjoy a moment on the water. [RAYNA SWANSON]

Sleep. The gentle rocking of the kayak always put my daughter to sleep. When we got back to the beach, if she was still asleep, I would secure the kayak onshore, lay the backpacking chair out flat in the kayak's cockpit, flip up the headrest of her PFD, and slide her down till she was lying flat on the chair. Then I would put some stroller netting over the cockpit to keep the bugs off. I would leave the stern of the boat in the water so she would still be gently rocked. Those were the best naps ever!

Sea Kayaking with Toddlers

Toddlers who can sit still do well in kayaks. Your child will sit in front of you, and depending on the size of your cockpit and length of your arms, your child will sit either forward of your paddle or right against your chest.

Safety. Practice holding your child and pretend to paddle and brace yourself on the beach before you get into the water. Going out in a pool or small lake to practice is also a good idea.

If you time your paddle around naptime, you will limit your toddler's awake time, when he or she is more likely to rock the boat—literally! A large cockpit is ideal: the child can sit forward of your paddle and hang onto the top of your cockpit. When the toddler falls asleep, just slide him or her down between your knees to nap.

Play. Give them activities! Provide your toddler with an inexpensive pair of binoculars to play with. Have them be on the lookout for whales, salmon jumping, or eagles flying overhead. It is also fun to sing. You can tie small floating toys to a string and the string to side of the boat. Toddlers like to throw the toys out and pull them back in. Choose a length of string that will not interfere with your paddling.

Sea Kayaking with Preschoolers

Preschool-aged children are old enough to sit alone in the cockpit of a double or triple kayak if the adult in the stern is strong enough to paddle the boat alone.

When our kids were preschool-age, we made a simple paddle from polyvinyl chloride (PVC) plastic piping for the handle and acrylic sheeting for the blade. We used fiberglass to secure the blade to the handle. The resulting paddle was just the right size for a three to five year old to practice paddling. It was also ineffectual enough to not slow down the boat with any drag. In other

The gentle rocking of the kayak always lulled my kids to sleep. [JEN AIST]

words, the kids could paddle all they wanted without moving any water.

CANOEING

Canoeing is very popular with young families, probably because it is easy to throw in the gear and the kids and go. For most children, though, the real fun starts when you hit the shore and they can run free, so try to keep your paddling time short and onshore breaks frequent.

Generally, it is advised to position the children in the center of the boat. If you have two adults in the canoe, you can put one child in front of the bow paddler, who is usually, but not necessarily, mom. Really young kids need tending on the boat, so the adult in the stern will need to do all the paddling at times.

With fishnet in place on the lifelines, and wearing their PFDs, these kids can safely enjoy some sun on the deck of their sailboat. [JENNIFER GORDON]

Never tether children to the canoe. In the event that it capsizes, you want your child to float up to the surface of the water, not be trapped underneath the canoe.

Canoeing with Infants

Logistically, canoeing with babies is easier than kayaking because there's no cockpit to restrict positioning. Again, a few keys to a successful trip:

Safety. Child-sized portable backpacking chairs or closed-cell sleeping pads (which you don't have to inflate) make a nice nest to place your baby on. If your baby uses a pacifier, be sure to use a leash on the pacifier so you don't lose it overboard.

Food. Young babies who may need to nurse frequently are easiest to handle in front of mom in the bow of the boat. You don't want to have to turn around to grab your baby and risk tipping the boat. Although it's not the easiest thing to do, you can breastfeed while wearing your PFD. Make sure it isn't too tight on your chest.

Sleep. Time your paddle around nap times. Ideally, the baby will be awake when you leave shore, want to interact with you for a bit, then sleep for a couple hours.

Canoeing with Toddlers

Toddlers typically take well to canoeing, but they like to stand up in the canoe and reach out to see and touch the water. The trouble with this is that leaning over to touch the water can easily result in the toddler going *into* the water. You can't blame toddlers for wanting to play with the water. And their heavy heads are just the height of the side of the boat, so it doesn't take much to tip the canoe's balance.

Safety. Some canoeists lean the canoe over to the side a bit so the toddler can easily see the water. Children tend to move around less in this position, too. From the shore, it looks as though the canoe might tip over, but it is perfectly safe with an experienced paddler—probably safer than the child leaning out of the canoe.

Food. Have a variety of snacks at the ready. Pack snacks that don't involve a lot of trash to keep track of. I keep a resealable plastic bag in my snack pack to put banana peels and wrappers in.

Sleep. Toddlers will undoubtedly want to nap in the canoe. Make a nice nest, just as you would for an infant, on the floor of the canoe using closed-cell foam pads or folded-out camp chairs. Pay attention to the amount of sun on your child; an umbrella can provide some shade. If bugs are a problem on the water, shield your napping child with bug netting.

Play. Entertaining a toddler in a canoe isn't much different from doing so in a kayak, except that you have more room in a canoe. Tie floating toys to the gunwales and thwarts for kids to throw out and retrieve. Some kids really like to drag a small fishing net in the water. An older toddler could even use a child-sized fishing rod (don't worry; these come without the hooks).

Canoeing with Preschoolers

By preschool age, most children are ready to start experimenting with a canoe paddle of their own. Remember, preschoolers aren't paddling to move the canoe so much as to get a feel for paddling.

> **TIPS & TRICKS**
>
> Start out young paddlers with lightweight plastic paddles sold with the cheap inflatable boats at discount stores. Their light weight and size make them ideal for young kids.

Play. I've heard from many canoeing families that dropping rocks into the water from the canoe is a favorite pastime. Before they launch, fill up a bucket with small rocks and have them ready. A rule about dropping and not throwing the rocks would be beneficial. Bubble blowing, wildlife viewing, fishing, and journaling are all great activities for canoeing preschoolers, too.

RAFTING

Most rafters advise sticking to Class I and occasionally Class II rivers with young children. White-water rafting on rivers with higher classification is generally not advised with babies. White-water fans may have to wait till the kids are older to bring them along. Or consider base camping along the river where a couple adults can stay onshore and play with the kids around camp while you go out for a day raft trip.

You also must know your own skill level and not exceed it without a knowledgeable guide—especially with your baby on board.

Planning a Raft Trip

Make sure you know your river. What is an easy float one month could have some dangerous currents after a good rain or big snowmelt near the headwaters. Quality guidebooks are available for most recreational rivers in the United States. Read them. Always talk to locals who know the river before you set out.

Memorial Day Weekend a few years back, we planned a river rafting trip with several other families. The plan was to camp Friday night and hit the river on Saturday.

The section of the river we chose usually made for an easy afternoon float. This weekend, though, the rain wouldn't let up, and the river rose higher and higher. The adults scoped out the river and made the decision to stay on land. Luckily, we had plenty of contingency plans in case rafting didn't work out. We biked, hiked up to a glacier, and went through a lot of sidewalk chalk at the campground.

SAFETY TIP

Always be prepared *not* to go on the water when you plan a boating trip.

While you are planning your rafting trip at home, scope the map closely for good pullouts along the shoreline for breaks and campsites. Mark those you want to check out in person. When you are actually on the river, pull over at these spots and make a note on your map for future trips.

Teach children to stay low when getting on a raft. [JEN AIST]

Safety

As with all other types of boating, the rules about wearing PFDs at all times and not tethering children to the raft apply. Catarafts are somewhat more stable than traditional rafts, but once your child is walking, the traditional raft is the way to go.

When you are planning where everyone will sit, consider sun, rain, and sleep. Plan a system to shield children from the sun. In some cases, your only option will be to have each child wear a wide-brimmed hat with sunglasses and sunscreen. Other times, you may be able to prop an umbrella to provide shade. The same goes for raingear: sometimes the kids will wear their own; other times you may be able to prop an umbrella for shelter. Rafts get pretty wet, so remember to dress your child in all synthetics, even on sunny days.

Teresa, who regularly fished on rivers from a raft, had twin girls. She secured two single jogging stroller chassis to either end of the cataraft, and fitted the strollers with infant sling attachments so the girls were comfortable. The front mesh kept out bugs, and the top shaded them on sunny or rainy days.

Stay on the river long enough, and kids will doze off to sleep. They are usually content curling up on a nice pile of dry bags and using the head support of their PFD as a pillow. When Teresa's girls got older, she set up a small pop-up tent on the bow to provide them a shady, bug-free spot to rest and read books while the parents fished.

EXCEPTIONAL CHILDREN

"Whether you think that you can or that you can't, you're right."
—Henry Ford

*E*veryone has a need to connect with nature, regardless of how they are able to interact with it. Children with all sorts of special needs can be taken into wild places, with some creativity and tips from parents who have gone before you.

For instance, deaf babies learn about the world through their eyes and their touch, so bring your baby close to interesting things in nature. Let her touch leaves and feel them crinkle in her hands. Use your expressions to communicate surprise, interest, and other emotions. Deaf babies (and newly walking toddlers) can be a bit more unbalanced on their feet than their hearing friends—our center of balance is housed in our ears and, if damaged, can affect balance—so offer a supportive hand when traveling over new terrain.

Children with visual impairments connect with the natural world in a more intimate way than seeing children do. Their heightened awareness of sounds makes them excellent birders, for instance. Many guides are available to help you learn bird calls and songs. Even very young children can learn to identify birds and other animals by sound.

Children with emotional disturbances benefit greatly from time outside. Activities such as rock climbing and backpacking can serve as huge self-esteem boosters for young children. Kids as young as three can be fitted for a climbing harness. Setting children up for an achievable challenge is a monumental aid. I have seen kids who normally are reserved and communicate negatively about themselves blossom in the wilderness. Nature is a wonderful neutralizer and balancer that can bring out the best in anyone.

In writing this chapter, I interviewed dozens of professionals and parents about their experiences taking children with special needs into the backcountry. I asked what advice they felt was the most important to pass on. While I expected to hear tips on adapting gear or ideal locations for adventures, what I heard over and over again is how much these families enjoy their trips. Their advice to parents of children with any disability considering a camping trip is simple: "Just do it."

While it is impossible to provide specific adaptations to accommodate every disability for every wilderness activity, this chapter offers some general suggestions. If there is one thing I have learned in twenty years of parent education, it is that parents know their children best. Combine some general, practical tips with your specialized knowledge of your children's abilities, and any parent can design a wilderness activity for any child.

GETTING THEM MOVING

My stepsister and brother-in-law have two great kids who love to play in the wilderness. They have camped, skiied, biked, and hiked whenever they could since the kids were babies.

Yet their youngest son has hereditary spastic paraplegia, a condition that makes it increasingly difficult for him to support his weight independently. Being the strong,

Shortened trekking poles keep this hiker on the trail. [BROOKE BANKS]

spirited kid that he is, he isn't about to stay home or go into the woods in a baby jogger. However, none of the youth trekking poles on the market are short enough for a four-year-old.

Using some creativity, his mom found an adult telescoping trekking pole that when compressed and locked in position is just the right height for him. The poles give him the extra support he needs while looking cool at the same time. This is a great example of the spirit of getting into the backcountry with exceptional children.

On the Trail

Toddlers with limited mobility can be carried in backpacks or soft-sided carriers. Preschoolers can be carried, but their weight and size may limit your hike. As the story about my stepsister demonstrates, adult trekking poles can be collapsed and used as poles for preschoolers and even toddlers. Poles with two adjustment points will get shorter than those with just one. Make sure the poles will lock in the collapsed position.

Trail developers are actively working with the special needs community to create durable nonasphalt surfaces that are respectful to the environment and compatible with wheelchairs, walkers, and baby strollers and joggers. Trail developers also are reducing the grade of these trails, to make pushing or self-propelling a wheelchair or stroller uphill possible. Trails that meet the criteria defined by the Americans with Disabilities Act are clearly labeled "handicap accessible" and can be found on the Internet or by contacting local trail authorities.

Toddlers with limited mobility can be pushed or pulled in jogging strollers or bike trailers on such trails. Preschoolers can be pushed in a jogging stroller as well, but the heavier the child, the harder it is to turn the stroller. Some specialized jogging strollers are designed specifically for heavier children; the axles are better suited to the weight, and they often have more substantial tires as well. Don't refer to the jogger as a "baby" jogger if you're using it with preschoolers. Just call it a jogger. Some kids won't care what you call it, but others certainly will. Spokes 'n Motion makes a specialized wheelchair called a Hippocampe that can easily travel over beaches, trails, snow, and rock. It can even go into lakes, oceans, and swimming pools.

TIPS & TRICKS

For a cheaper option than purchased trekking poles, try cutting down old ski poles. Using a vise grip, remove the pole's handle. Then, with a pipe cutter, make the adjustment to the metal pole. Keep in mind that these poles are tapered, so you can't cut too much away. When you are done, reattach the handle. My kids like to decorate their poles with stickers.

On the Water

Boating is a great option for kids with limited or no mobility. The rhythmic rocking of a kayak or canoe can be especially calming and centering. The personal flotation device provides some upper-body support. If additional support is needed, look into foam wedges that you can place strategically around the child. Do not strap the child to the boat; do not tape paddles to the child's hands. In an emergency, you want the child to be free of the boat.

All children love playing in tents. [KEVIN KEELER]

Janet Zeller had been canoeing for more than thirty years when an injury left her a quadriplegic with limited use of her hands. However, she continues to canoe and kayak, co-authoring *Canoeing and Kayaking for Persons with Disabilities.* "Paddling is freedom from my wheelchair and a sense of being equal on the water that is unique to paddle sports," she writes. "A body that is so uncooperative on land becomes part of a sleek craft gliding through the water; there are no barriers to stop me."

Zeller eloquently puts into words what many children feel when they take their first ride in a canoe or kayak. Boating also gives freedom to the whole family. It is a sport that everyone can enjoy, regardless of age or ability.

On Horseback

Dozens of outstanding therapeutic riding programs exist across the United States. These programs use horses to connect children with nature and with themselves. They are appropriate for children with an array of disabilities including autism, muscular dystrophy, multiple sclerosis, paralysis, Down syndrome, attention deficit disorder, amputation, and cerebral palsy. The benefits of therapeutic riding are numerous.

Horses can also be a gateway into the backcountry for children with disabilities. More and more trails are handicapped accessible, but the vast majority of backcountry trails are not usable with baby joggers or wheelchairs. Horse packing can get children with limited mobility into areas that would otherwise be totally inaccessible.

SPECIAL TOILETING CONCERNS

Keeping special-needs toileting materials sanitary in the woods can be a challenge. Try using the diaper-sack technique described in the Dirt chapter, which helps keep everything you need clean and easy to find in an instant.

Lori's daughter Shae was born with spina bifida and hydrocephalus; Shae does not have bladder control and needs to be catheterized every two to four hours. Yet Lori first brought Shae out camping when she was just six weeks old. Lori had a bag dedicated to toileting that included catheters, baby wipes, iodine, latex gloves, a change of clothing, plastic bags for used or soiled items, and a pad to place under Shae during the catheterization. When packing for a trip, Lori packed double the quantity that she normally used at home. She felt the wipes and pad, in particular, were invaluable in maintaining some level of cleanliness.

Lori's tips for cleanliness are helpful whether your child needs to be catheterized or not—and her example of a can-do spirit is an inspiration.

MEDICATIONS
Maintaining medication schedules requires some planning. To keep meds clean and make dispensing them easier, pack them in daily packs and double-bag them to keep them dry. If you are traveling on or near water, pack them in a dry bag to ensure they don't get wet.

Always bring a couple days' worth of extra medications in case you are unable to get home on schedule due to changing weather or other unexpected circumstances.

Watches and personal digital assistants (PDAs such as iPods) can be programmed to signal medication times; you can use a small notepad to record medication administration times.

PLANNING A SUCCESSFUL TRIP
Parents can frequently, and understandably, be overwhelmed by their children's diagnoses as babies, and the thought of bringing their special-needs baby just to the grocery store can be a bit daunting. But they shouldn't forgo the outdoors; just as nature is regenerative to children, it is to parents as well. These steps can help you have a successful trip:
1. Think about where you want to go and what you want to do: boating, car camping, backpacking, etc.
2. Make a list of the challenges, both actual (medications, mobility limitations, lack of sensation in the feet, etc.) and potential, depending on your child's situation.
3. Go through the list one by one and troubleshoot solutions: look online for resources, talk with friends, join chat rooms.
4. Plan your trip well, then head out; take notes and create tips of your own for your next trip and for sharing with others.

We need nature just as much as our kids do. Know that you are not alone; some amazing people are blazing the trail for you all across the country. As Lori said about Shae, "I wanted to normalize her life as much as possible. Camping was important because children should do that. As much extra work as it was, it was worth it!"

PART IV

Connecting with Nature

**Activities Around Camp | Wildlife Activities |
Nature Activities**

ACTIVITIES AROUND CAMP

"The joy of looking and comprehending is nature's most beautiful gift."
—Albert Einstein

Before families set out on their first adventures with their kids, they want to know how to sleep with babies on the trail and how to carry them on the trail. But often they don't think about what to do with the kids once they're at camp—until, that is, the family returns from that first trip. Then they have tons of questions about how to entertain kids and keep them safe around the tent or cabin.

One of the biggest differences between camping with adults and camping with young ones is the "down time." With adults, you hike, climb, or boat all day, then arrive at camp. You set up your tent, kitchen, and campsite, then sit down, relax, and watch the sun go down. Fast-forward to camping with kids: You hike, climb, or boat all day, taking frequent stops to feed, change, and entertain kids, then arrive at camp. One adult sets up the tent alone while the other takes care of the baby. Then you switch roles and get the kitchen set up and dinner going. Then you position yourselves strategically around camp to allow for maximum supervision of your toddler while you try to rest your feet for the next day.

Alex took his six-month-old son out on an overnight backpacking trip. He had a lot of fun, but he really had a hard time with tasks like setting up the tent. When I asked him if he would do it again, he gave me an enthusiastic yes. But he might want to bring more help next time; his wife just delivered triplets!

INFANT ACTIVITIES
Imagine for a moment that a rock just landed from another planet. Think about how you would approach the rock. You might be cautious at first, not knowing whether it

was safe to interact with. You might just look at it from a distance or use a stick to turn it around. Then you might pick it up and perhaps smell it. As soon as you felt confident it wasn't going to harm you, you would likely begin experimentation, putting the object through a battery of tests such as dropping it to test its density. Did it break right away or stay solid? What does it taste like? Is it magnetic? Can it be used as a tool?

This is the same investigative process that infants use on everyday objects. They pick things up, look them over, bring them to their mouth, and, like good scientists, repeat their experiments again and again. That way, they get really valid results. Start thinking of your baby as a scientist, and suddenly the smallest things are superinteresting.

This junior naturalist is taking great joy in checking out a stick. [LIZZY DONOVAN]

Make sure your baby gets plenty of time to sit on the ground and explore. Many families get stuck in the rut of staying in the tent all day with crawling babies. It really is OK for them to crawl outside in the dirt! If the ground is too hard and rocky for their knees, they won't crawl on it; they will just sit and explore right where they are.

You can also bring a blanket and create a softer environment for a baby to crawl on. However, most parents of crawling babies know that the baby will just crawl off the blanket as soon as you spread it out on the ground.

Talk to your baby about what you see, what you hear, what you feel. Help him or her learn the vocabulary of nature to give context to camping experiences. Use descriptive words like "soft," "poky," and "fragrant" to describe the world around you. Guide your baby's hand to gently touch plants and rocks and such. Remember, for your baby this could be the first time he or she has seen or touched these things.

Toys

By crawling age, many babies want a small toy or two on camping trips. When choosing a toy, pick one that can get dirty. For times when your baby is riding in a backpack or child carrier, choose toys that can be attached to the pack with toy links so you don't lose them.

Photo Books

Take a lot of pictures on your trip so you can create a simple book for your baby to look at again and again after the trip. Internet photo sites can help you make easy, great-looking digital albums. Keep the text simple—just a few words per page, such as "Our tent" or "Hiking home." Your baby will love reading the book and reliving the memories.

TODDLER ACTIVITIES

Young walkers are busy little people. Encourage plenty of unstructured exploration time. Exploration time is an opportunity for toddlers to follow their gaze and set out to touch and feel. Follow behind your little explorer, asking open-ended questions ("I wonder what would happen if . . . ?") and making affirming statements about what they are experiencing ("I like the way you are being so gentle with that flower!"). For more ideas, see the Nature Activities chapter.

Toys

Kids this age really like collecting things and carrying them around. A simple plastic bucket and shovel often are the only toys you need to bring. Try not to fall into the trap of bringing all the toys from home. Trust me; they really don't need them. Young toddlers will be just fine with a couple of toys and some board books to read.

Bring one or two favorite books to read at bedtime or on rainy days when you might be stuck in the tent, cabin, or camper. Some families bring lightweight music-playing devices with children's music or stories.

If you are car camping, sidewalk chalk can provide hours of fun. It is cheap, lightweight, and easy to clean up. You can use it to draw pictures as well as to make rubbings on trees or leaves. You can also draw a lazy trail for kids to follow as a balance beam.

I also use chalk to create boundaries for kids. When cars are driving through the campground, I like to keep the kids at our campsite. A line at the edge of the driveway helps children know where they can go and where they can't.

Music

If someone in your group plays a guitar, harmonica, or other instrument, ask that person to bring the instrument if it's practical. There is nothing like live music in the woods! If you don't know any hiking musicians, you can always sing.

I have such wonderful memories of sitting around the campfire and singing songs. Some songs I liked so much, I sang them to my babies while they were falling asleep. And now my kids sing these same songs to their dolls and friends' babies when they come over to visit. See the Resources section for some links to camp songs.

Journals

My youngest daughter liked to "journal" when she was a toddler. She would find a quiet space to sit and write pages of "notes" in her little notebook with her colored pencils. It was just scribbles, but she took it very seriously, as if she were writing a novel. Notebooks from Write in the Rain really do hold up to writing in the rain. We've brought regular paper, but it always gets soggy, which frustrates children. I leave crayons at

A simple swing can be the perfect way to spend an afternoon in camp. [TOM TWIGG]

home, unless I'm car camping in cooler temperatures, because they melt and make a really big mess.

One of my kids left a crayon in a pocket, which ended up going through the wash. Almost everything in the whole load was stained with melted crayon—which, of course, was red. Even worse, it went through the dryer. It took me hours to scrub out the crayon residue with solvent. The whole experience soured me on crayons for quite some time!

TIPS & TRICKS

Put together a journaling kit in a resealable plastic bag. Include a waterproof notepad (they come in many sizes and styles) and a set of colored pencils. You might decorate the outside of the bag with a marking pen.

PRESCHOOL ACTIVITIES

By preschool age, children are ready for more complex nature exploration. Because they have longer attention spans and increased capacity for learning, this is a great time to start exposing kids to the wondrous field of science. Bring along some simple scientific instruments, such as these:

- magnifying glass
- pair of tweezers
- bug nets to catch (and release) butterflies and moths and to skim creeks and lakes for minnows
- plastic buckets or jars to collect water, minnows, rocks, spiders, and all sorts of other objects

These items are perfect examples of what experts call open-ended toys: toys that can be used in a million different creative ways. When the toy doesn't directly drive the play, it is open-ended. Open-

Journaling is a wonderful activity for any child. [JEN AIST]

ended toys and play foster learning, creativity, and problem solving—all great qualities to nurture in our children.

If space and weight allow, bring along guidebooks and field guides to help extend their learning about the environment you're visiting.

Toys and Games

Preschoolers might be happy with something to throw, such as a ball or flying disk, a simple floating toy if your trip is near water, or a kite.

Old standbys such as playing cards and dice come in handy when it's raining. My kids like to play "speed Scrabble" with just the letter tiles and not the game board; you can also purchase a travel version of this game.

Children will group together and create their own games outdoors. [JEN AIST]

WILDLIFE ACTIVITIES

"Nothing exists for itself alone, but only in relation to other forms of life."

—Charles Darwin

When my family goes on a hike in the woods, a paddle in the ocean, or a ridgeline walk, we are always on the lookout for wildlife. Watching animals in their own habitat is always a special treat. We scan the trails for footprints, scat (droppings), or tufts of fur left behind on branches. We look for bear scratches on trees and bones left after a kill. When we find something, we jot a note down on the map with the date of sighting and the species. On subsequent trips, we enjoy looking back over our maps to remember the animals we have seen in those places.

Preschoolers enjoy studying tracks. You can find many great tracking guides for specific areas. Whenever you see a footprint in the ground, stop and study it. See if you and your children can figure out which direction the animal was traveling and how old the track is. It isn't as important to know all the answers as it is to try to discover the tracks.

TIPS & TRICKS

My children and I make up stories about the animal's tracks. We imagine who had walked with the feet that made those tracks and what that creature might have thought as it was going down that trail.

FOLLOW WILDLIFE GUIDELINES

Urban dwellers sometimes think that packs of drooling carnivores are lurking around every cactus and tree in the wilderness, waiting for a tender young hiker to come along. In reality, attacks from wild animals are extremely rare. The vast majority of wildlife you and your family might see in the wilderness has no interest in you at all. Big or small, furry or scaly, in the water or air or on land, wild animals would prefer never to interact with humans. Chances are that the average wild creature has had far more sightings of humans than we have of them.

Find out what wildlife you are likely to encounter before your trip. Good sources of information include local offices of the Bureau of Land Management, state departments of fish and wildlife, state parks, U.S. Forest Service ranger stations, and National Park Service visitor information centers. These agencies all have websites loaded with information.

The actual wildlife you encounter will vary depending on where your adventures

This budding naturalist is all ready to spot any creature from the trail. [JONATHAN DITTO]

take you, but the principles of how to safely and respectfully interact with wild creatures remain the same. The Alaska Department of Fish and Game, Division of Wildlife Conservation, provides the following guidelines for wildlife viewing, which hold true across the country:

- Give wildlife plenty of space. Binoculars and spotting scopes allow you to view wildlife without getting too close. Approach wildlife slowly, quietly, and indirectly. Always give animals an avenue for retreat.

- Try to view animals without changing their behavior. Avoid using calls or devices that attract wildlife. Resist the temptation to throw rocks to see a flock of birds fly. Remember—harassing wildlife is illegal.

A simple scientific tool like a hand lens really enhances the experience for kids. [KIMMER BALL]

- Be respectful of nesting and denning areas, rookeries, and calving grounds. Well-meaning but intrusive visitors may cause animal parents to flee, leaving young animals vulnerable to the elements or predators. Stay on designated trails whenever possible.

- Leave "orphaned" or sick animals alone. Young animals that appear alone usually have parents waiting nearby.

- Restrain pets or leave them at home. They may startle, chase, or even kill wildlife.

- Let animals eat their natural foods. Sharing your sandwich may get animals hooked on handouts; it may even harm their digestive systems. These animals may eventually lose their fear of cars, campers, or even poachers.

- Learn to recognize signs of alarm. These are sometimes subtle. Leave if an animal shows them.

Animal behaviors vary from place to place, so ask the local officials about proper animal safety in that area for yourself and your children. For example, where bears have lost their fear of humans, you will be advised to respond to an approaching bear very differently from an area where bears are still completely wild. I know a lot about Alaska bears, but if I were camping in Yosemite, I would talk to the local officials about bear habits in that environment. Likewise, I know how to handle myself in Alaska around a group of moose in the fall during rut (mating season). But I'm not so comfortable with a herd of elk in Canada. Just as people and their behaviors are a bit different throughout the world, so it is with animals. Educate yourself before you go.

Bring along some nets so your children can discover creatures along the shore without handling—or harming—them. [JEN AIST]

LEARN TO OBSERVE

Viewing wildlife is always a special thrill. I could sit on a ridge and watch caribou all day long. I like to watch for sea lions and sea otters from my kayak. And when I get the rare opportunity to sneak a peek at a lynx, I am all adrenaline.

Very young children have a slightly different perspective, though. Their true joy is in watching the microenvironments all around us. They can sit and study the tiny creatures on the underside of a rock all afternoon.

I was out hiking recently with a friend and her two-year-old in Wyoming's Yellowstone National Park. We stopped on the path, along with a herd of other people, to catch a glimpse of a grizzly bear that was sleeping. We could really only see its paws and its back. Kids and adults alike with binoculars were all clamoring, jostling to catch

With wet hands to protect the fish, this little guy can check out a small fry up close without harming it. [JEN AIST]

the best view. This was safe bear viewing at its best.

My friend's little two year old and my six-year-old son had found something far more exciting to watch, however. They spotted a tiny bug climbing around a wild rosebud. They followed this little creature with as much enthusiasm as they could muster. My son looked up and said, "We can see him and we don't even need binoculars!" I had to smile.

Wonderful things happen when your fifteen-month-old toddler discovers small life forms. Remember, young children are amazing scientists always on the lookout for another great discovery. An hour with an earthworm is quality lab time. Encourage your little ones to touch and explore.

Sometimes, though, little fingers can poke and squeeze a bit too hard for some little animals—if this happens, encourage your scientist to "look with your eyes." After all, we want children to develop an appreciation for living things, not smashed things.

Because infants and toddlers use their mouths to learn about the world, you might want to watch for worms, bugs, and such going down the hatch. Chances are your child will swallow a worm or two in early childhood. While I don't encourage children to eat bugs, I wouldn't worry too much about it happening, either.

Even before your child can talk, start asking open-ended questions about the animal your child is looking at. For example, in the worm lab, you could ask questions like these: "How does it feel?" "Where do think it is going?" "I wonder what the worm is thinking?" Learning happens in the process, not the answer. Asking questions such as these will keep your child's learning process active.

When children learn more about, and interact more with, the world around them, they connect with their surroundings on a level that can't be broken. And when you are connected with something, you will protect it. This is our gift as parents to our children and our planet alike.

NATURE ACTIVITIES

"Study nature, love nature, stay close to nature. It will never fail you."
—Frank Lloyd Wright

Such fun can be had playing in the dirt. There is something liberating about knowing that you can have a fun and meaningful experience without any planning and with few—if any—purchased materials. I've often sat in meetings that seemed as though a few of the adults could really benefit from some dirt time. This chapter is all about fun, easy activities you can do outdoors with your child at just about any age. I hope you get a chance to feel the power of play.

PROP-FREE ACTIVITIES

Alphabet hike. If your preschooler is learning to read and recognize the sounds of letters, try this game. As you hike along, look for things in nature that start with each letter of the alphabet, starting with A. For example, "A is for ant; B is for blue sky; C is for cat hole;" et cetera.

Cloud tales. Have your children lie down on their backs and imagine the clouds as different characters in a story. You can create the beginning, then let your children add to the story.

Count the sounds. While hiking, sitting around camp, or relaxing on the boat, ask your children to try to count and identify each sound they hear. Listen carefully; you might be surprised just how many different things you hear.

Night hike. When the campground is quiet and the campfire is out, it's a good time to take a night hike. Bring along a flashlight or headlamp if you like, but try to leave it off. Children often have fears about the dark and night in general. Sitting somewhere quietly on the trail after dark and listening to nature can help to alleviate some of these fears. In a whisper, talk about how the same animals that you saw earlier in the day are getting ready for bed just like you are. As your eyes adjust to the darkness, look for ants, squirrels, or birds. Try to count how many different sounds you can hear.

ACTIVITIES USING NATURE'S PROPS

Building dams. Small creeks are wonderful labs for learning the finer points of hydrodynamics. Encourage children to build dams and find out what happens. If you are lucky enough to pass a beaver dam on the trail, stop and study how the beavers did it. Just don't practice cutting down trees with your own teeth.

   Collecting wild berries and edible plants. Teach your children never to eat a wild berry or other plant without checking with an adult first. Teach your children—even the toddlers—how to identify safe plants, then together pick wild edibles such as berries. Eat as you go, or bring along an empty water bottle to collect your findings for a snack later on.

Watermelon berries are a tasty discovery on a hike. [JEN AIST]

Nature provides children with materials for all sorts of creations. [TOM TWIGG]

Drawing in the mud or sand. Show your children how to use a stick as a writing instrument to make squiggles, lines, and dots in the mud or sand. Preschool children can play tic-tac-toe this way.

Making grass whistles. Take a long, wide piece of grass and hold it taut between your thumbs. With your other fingers clasped together, blow through your thumbs and see what different sounds you can make. Now have your kids try it. Does it work with dry grass? Does it work with skinny grass?

Making stick or rock art. Prompt your children to arrange sticks, rocks, or both together in various patterns. Have them try simple shapes to begin with. Toddlers often like to make long lines, whereas preschoolers tend to create more complex patterns, and kindergarteners will often spell out their names. Suggest they use some leaves, pinecones, or other natural elements for details.

Making a sundial. At camp, show your children how to draw a simple sundial in the dirt and plug a stick upright into the middle. Ask them to make observations about the direction of the shadow throughout the day.

Skipping stones. To avoid injuries from flying rocks, instruct your children to

Sometimes you need a helping hand from your big sister when crossing big logs. [JEN AIST]

always keep their toes touching the edge of the water (provided the water has a gentle shore) and to never throw a stone if someone is in front of them. For toddlers, this is more like tossing stones, but it's just as fun.

NEARLY PROP-FREE ACTIVITIES

Dry, dry, wet. This is the hot-weather version of the classic "Duck, Duck, Goose" game. Everyone sits in a circle; the person who is It walks around the outside of the circle with a wet bandanna saying, "Dry, dry, dry." Finally the person who is It squeezes water from the bandanna onto the head of someone sitting in the circle and says, "Wet." The wet person now runs around the outside of the circle while the person who is It races to sit in the empty spot. Whoever reaches the empty spot second is now It. For more fun, you can change the words to "Deer, Deer, Fish," "Bear, Bear, River Otter," or other land and water animal names.

Fundanas games. Fundanas are hiking games printed on bandannas—a piece of clothing that's great to have around camp or on a hike anyway. There's Bug Bingo, Desert Bingo, and dozens more, including a whole line of games specifically designed for preschool children.

Nature rubbings. Have your children place some journal paper from their journaling kits over a leaf or a tree trunk, and, using their colored pencils, make gentle strokes to create a textural image of the object. You can also have your children collect fallen leaves and flower petals to include in their nature journals.

Scavenger hunts. Make a list of items to find in nature, either writing it down in words or pictures or reciting it orally, depending on the resources you have and the ages of your children. Include items on your list such as "things an ant would like to play with" or "items to create a home for a worm." You can also include "small, medium, and large rocks," "leaves," or such. Then have your children race to see who can gather the items the quickest. More complex lists might require a bucket or day pack to gather the items in.

THE BEST NATURE ACTIVITY

Whether you push, pull, or pack your child on a path, a trail, an ocean, a lake, or a river, I hope you and your babes begin a tradition of connecting with nature fully and frequently. We are all well suited to wild spaces and have so much to gain by spending time in them. The best nature activity is just going, so get out there and have a fabulously fantastic time.

BIBLIOGRAPHY

Alaska Department of Fish and Game. *Alaska Project WILD: Early Childhood Curriculum* Anchorage: Division of Wildlife Conservation—Wildlife Education, 2004.

Arnosky, Jim. *Secrets of a Wildlife Watcher: A Beginner's Field Guide.* Sag Harbor, N.Y.: Beech Tree Books, 1991.

Best Hikes with Kids series. Seattle: The Mountaineers Books.

Cornell, Joseph. *Sharing the Joy of Nature: Nature Activities for All Ages.* Nevada City, Calif.: Dawn Publications, 1989.

_____. *Sharing Nature with Children.* Nevada City, Calif.: Dawn Publications, 1998.

Gicle, Judith. "Raising Kids Who Care." *Seattle's Child,* January 14, 2009.

Grahn, P., F. Martensson, B. Lindblad, P. Nilsson, and A. Ekinan. "Ute pa Dagis." *Stad & Land,* 1997. p. 145.

Hahn, Jeffery, Phil Pellitteri, and Donald Lewis. *Wasp and Bee Control.* St. Paul: University of Minnesota Cooperative Extension, 2009.

Isaac, Jeff, P.A.-C., and Peter Goth, M.D. *The Outward Bound Wilderness First-Aid Handbook.* New York: Lyons and Burford, 1991.

Kraiker, Rolf, and Debra Kraiker. *Cradle to Canoe: Camping and Canoeing with Children.* Erin, Ont.: Boston Mills Press, 1999.

Lite, Jordan. "BPA Study: Plastic Chemical is Unhealthy for Children and Other Living Things." *Scientific American,* September 16, 2008.

Louv, Richard. *Last Child in the Woods: Saving Our Children from Nature-Deficit Disorder.* Chapel Hill, N.C.: Algonquin Paperbacks, 2008.

Miller, Dorcas. *Backcountry Cooking Deck: 50 Recipes for Camp & Trail.* Seattle: The Mountaineers Books, 2008.

Prater, Yvonne et al. *Beyond Gorp: Favorite Foods from Outdoor Experts.* Seattle: The Mountaineers Books, 2005.

Ross, Cindy, and Todd Gladfelter. *Kids in the Wild: A Family Guide to Outdoor Recreation.* Seattle: The Mountaineers Books, 1995.

Stonorov, Derek. *Living in Harmony with Bears.* Anchorage, Alaska: Alaska State Office of the National Audubon Society, 2000.

Ward, Jennifer. *I Love Dirt! 52 Activities to Help You and Your Kids Discover the Wonders of Nature.* New York: Random House, 2008.

Watson, Tom. *Kids Gone Paddlin': The Young Paddlers Guide to Having More Fun Outdoors.* Minneapolis, Minn.: Creative Publishing International, 2008.

Wilderness Medicine Institute. *Wilderness Medicine Handbook.* Lander, Wyo.: National Outdoor Leadership School, 2004.

RESOURCES

The lists below correspond to the book's chapters. Be sure to also check out www.babesinthewoods.info for reviews of outdoor gear and trails for families as well as downloadable gear lists and more.

Clothing

www.campmor.com. Campmor has some terrific deals on clothing and gear.

www.landsend.com. Lands End has been making infant and toddler wear for quite some time. Look closely at the designs; some of their clothes are better suited for backyard play than backcountry.

www.mec.ca. MEC is the Canadian version of REI. They have high-quality clothing and gear in all sizes.

www.molehillmtn.com. Molehill specializes in high-quality outdoor wear specifically designed for infants and children. They have a great selection, and their products hold up well to a lot of outdoor use.

www.patagonia.com. Patagonia has long been a leader in outdoor clothing. They also carry an extensive line of infant- and toddler-sized clothing.

www.puddlegear.com. Puddlegear makes high-quality chemical-free raingear for infants and children. Their stuff lasts forever.

www.rei.com. Recreational Equipment Inc. carries some infant- and a lot of child-sized gear. Check out their clearance section for some great deals.

www.upsideover.com. Upside Over is a general catalog website for outdoor gear for kids. They carry equipment as well as clothing and footwear.

Food

www.backpackerspantry.com. American Outdoor Products makes the Outback Oven, which is your ticket to baking brownies, pizza, bread, and more on the trail. They also carry an enormous assortment of dehydrated meals.

www.bottless.org. Bottless makes stainless-steel water bottles with sippy lid attachments.

www.crkt.com. Columbia River Knife & Tool company sells hundreds of different knives and tools.

www.innate-gear.com. Innate makes stainless-steel water bottles and insulated vacuum bottles. They have a toddler-sized water bottle with a sippy lid attachment.

www.katadyn.us. Katadyn has long been a leader in the water purification world. They make a great gravity-fed water filter perfect for family base camping.

www.kid-basix.com. Kid Basix makes the Safe Sippy and Safe Starter, stainless-steel water bottles with sippy lid attachments. The starter is designed to use with a bottle nipple for infants.

www.kleankanteen.com. Klean Kanteen makes stainless-steel water bottles, including toddler sizes with sippy lid attachments.

www.mountainsmith.com. Mountainsmith makes great packs in addition to the Modular Hauler system, which helps you organize your food and cooking gear on base-camp and car-camping trips.

www.steripen.com. The SteriPEN uses ultraviolet light to purify drinking water. It is small, lightweight, and easy to bring on any trip.

Sun

www.babybanz.com. Babybanz makes quality sunglasses for infants and children and also carries a line of sun protection clothing and earmuffs (for flying) for infants.

www.sundayafternoons.com. Sunday Afternoons has an incredible selection of extremely well-made hats for infants, toddlers, children, and adults.

www.sunprecautions.com. Sun Precautions makes toddler- and adult-sized sun protective clothing. They do not have an infant line.

www.sunsmart.com. The Cancer Council Victoria's (Australia) skin cancer prevention program is internationally recognized.

Bugs

www.allterrainco.com. All Terrain makes natural remedies for outdoor enthusiasts. They have a kid line that includes sunscreen and insect repellent.

www.buzzoffoutdoorwear.com. Buzz Off makes a whole line of mesh clothing for adults and children. They do not have infant sizes.

www.hylands.com. Hylands is a homeopathic company that makes Bug Bite, a fabulous anti-itch product.

Dirt

www.lnt.org. Leave No Trace—the leading authority on outdoor ethics—has a lot of good information on its website.

Sleep

www.bigagnes.com. The "Little Agnes Series" bag is designed to fit the sleeping pad into a pocket in the bag. Big Agnes also makes a double bag that works well for sleeping with your baby.

www.functionaldesign.net. Functional Design makes the sleeping bag doubler, which comes in two different sizes and weights.

www.kelty.com. Kelty makes a kid-sized bag; many Kelty products are carried at REI.

www.thenorthface.com. North Face makes several really nice kid-sized bags.

www.pacoutdoor.com. Pacific Outdoor Equipment makes child-sized sleeping pads and family-sized pads. They also make a child-sized backpacking chair.

www.7amenfant.com. 7 AM Enfant makes a high-quality baby foot muff to keep babies warm in a stroller or a bike trailer. A foot muff is similar to a sleeping bag with holes in the back to allow the straps from the carrier to pass through.

www.sierradesigns.com. Sierra Designs makes a fabulous youth bag in both 20 degree F and 40 degree F ratings.

www.slumberjack.com. Look in Slumberjack's "kids" section; they have one bag that can be extended for use as your child grows.

www.treklightgear.com. Treklight hammocks are lightweight, very packable, and tons of fun.

Safety

www.epa.gov/sunwise. The Environmental Protection Agency posts UV radiation forecasts for locations across the United States.

www.lightningsafety.noaa.gov. The National Weather Service's website is dedicated to educating the public about lightning safety.

www.nasar.org. The National Association for Search and Rescue web site is home to the Hug -A-Tree program.

www.nhc.noaa.gov. The National Hurricane Center website is managed by the National Weather Service. All warnings and forecasts are posted here.

www.wunderground.com. Weather Underground posts forecasts for cities all across the globe. It includes satellite pictures, humidity, dew point, windchill, UV, cloud cover, and more.

Child Carriers

www.thebabywearer.com. This forum is chock full of great research and tips about every baby carrier out there, plus discussion boards for all sorts of baby-wearing topics, including special needs kids.

www.cabinbaby.com. Cabin Baby is a fabulous pouch sling made by a local Alaskan family in many fabrics, including fleece.

www.deuterusa.com. Deuter makes some nice frame packs and a Kangakid carrier that converts a day pack into a carrier.

www.ergobabycarrier.com. Ergo, based in Hawaii, makes a high-quality baby carrier.

www.gypsymama.com. Wrapsody makes a fabulous water wrap for swimming.

www.kelty.com. Kelty has long been a leader in external frame baby backpacks.

www.mckinleykidz.com. McKinley Kidz, another local Alaskan family company, sells all types of soft baby carriers as well as vests and coats to wear over the baby.

www.mobywrap.com. Moby makes wraps in many different fabrics, including material with UPF.

www.suseskinder.com. Suse's Kinder sells a wide variety of baby-wearing coats, jackets, and vests.

Jogging Strollers and Bike Trailers, Trailer Bikes, and Bikes

www.babyjogger.com. Baby Jogger makes basic, well-built jogging strollers favored by runners for their extra-large wheels. They also make jogging strollers for large children.

www.bobgear.com. Bob strollers are versatile and adaptable to both trail and urban settings.

www.burley.com. Burley has been making fine bike trailers for a long time.

www.chariotcarriers.com. Chariot makes a child carrier system with attachments that convert the chassis into a jogging stroller or trailer.

Car Camping

www.ohranger.com. American Park Network's website, a comprehensive source of information on national parks and public lands, is very easy to navigate and contains great information.

www.reserveamerica.com. Reserve America has a fabulous wealth of information to find and reserve campgrounds and cabins in the United States.

Base Camping

www.bigagnes.com. Big Agnes makes some great family tents with huge vestibules.

www.kelty.com. Kelty makes a kid-sized bag as well as family tents; many Kelty products are carried at REI.

www.mountainhardwear.com. Mountain Hardwear caries a whole line of family tents that will stand up to the elements.

www.sierradesigns.com. Sierra Designs makes some quality family tents.

Backpacking

www.golite.com. Go Lite is the master when it comes to ultralight camping. And when you are carrying gear for a few folks, ultralight is good. They make many gender-specific backpacks for day and multiday trips.

www.mountainsmith.com. Mountainsmith makes packs for every occasion, including a well-built multiday pack for youth. Many of their packs are made from recycled materials as well.

www.ospreypacks.com. Osprey makes several outstanding multiday packs for children for when your junior hikers get a little bit older.

Boating

www.americanwhitewater.org. American Whitewater's mission is to conserve and restore America's white-water resources and enhance opportunities to enjoy them safely.

www.mtiadventurewear.com. MTI makes a large selection of PFDs for all ages.

www.salusmarine.com. Salus Marine makes the Bijoux baby PFD, which fits babies from 9 pounds and up.

Exceptional Children

www.deafkidskamp.com. Deaf Kids Kamp in Big Bear, California, is the only free, accredited camp specifically designed for deaf children west of the Mississippi.

www.mocsi.org/campeureka. Camp Eureka is a Montana-based natural history camp for nine- to fourteen-year-old children who are blind.

www.narha.org. North American Riding for the Handicapped Association is home to *Strides* journal and many additional great resources.

www.spokesnmotion.com. Spokes 'n Motion is home to adaptive sports equipment. They have a whole section of children's equipment, including the Hippocampe.

www.stridestherapeutic.com. Therapeutic Riding Center in Tarzana, California, has a wealth of information on its site.

Activities Around Camp

www.ultimatecampresource.com. Ultimate Camp Resource lists songs by type, such as "repeat after," "sentimental," or "classic." They also have campfire stories and skits.

CHECKLISTS

The Ten Essentials

Double-check this list before each trip (see also the Day Hiking chapter):

_____ Navigation: map and compass

_____ Sun protection: sunglasses and sunscreen

_____ Insulation (extra clothing)

_____ Illumination: headlamp or flashlight

_____ First-aid kit

_____ Fire: firestarter and lighter or matches

_____ Repair kit and tools: pocket knife

_____ Nutrition (extra food)

_____ Hydration (extra water)

_____ Emergency shelter: space blanket

CLOTHING CHECKLISTS

Base Layer

_____ 1 pair underwear per day plus 2 extra

_____ 2 pair socks per day plus 3 extra

_____ 2 sets lightweight wool, silk, nylon, or polypropylene tops and bottoms

Insulating Layer

_____ 2 cotton T-shirts per day

_____ lightweight fleece or wool long-sleeved top

_____ shorts

_____ zip-off pants (nylon)

_____ cotton pants

_____ 2 fleece pants (1 light, 1 heavy)

_____ hiking boots and/or tennis shoes

Outer Layer for Wet Conditions: Raingear

_____ lightweight wind or rain shell

_____ rain suit (one-piece) or raincoat and pants

_____ waterproof or -resistant hat

_____ waterproof or -resistant mittens

_____ 2–3 pair wool socks

_____ rain boots or water shoes

_____ umbrella

Outer Layer for Cold Conditions

_____ snow suit or bibs

_____ parka

_____ warm hat that covers ears well

_____ waterproof gloves or mittens

_____ 2 pair thin liner mittens or gloves

_____ 2–3 pair wool socks

_____ overboots or snowboots

_____ gaiters

_____ hand warmers, foot warmers, chest warmers

_____ lanolin, lip balm, petroleum jelly

_____ goggles or sunglasses

SUN PROTECTION CHECKLIST

____ UPF-treated, loose-fitting long-sleeved shirt and pants

____ lightweight windbreaker

____ wide-brimmed hat that covers neck and ears

____ lightweight wool socks

____ closed-toe and -heel sandals

____ sunscreen

____ sunglasses, case, leashes

____ umbrella

____ bandanna

BUG PROTECTION CHECKLIST

____ protective bug netting—a lot of it!

____ screened tent or shelter

____ gaiters

____ DEET-based insect repellent

____ non-DEET-based insect repellent

____ calamine lotion, cortisone cream

____ Benadryl or Zyrtec (check with pediatrician regarding antihistamines first)

DIRT PROTECTION CHECKLISTS
Diaper and Toilet Gear

____ 5 diapers per day plus 5 extra

____ wipes in a small plastic container

____ diaper cream

____ bucket for soiled diapers (extended base camp trip)

____ plastic bag for soiled diapers (short trip)

____ portable potty

____ toilet paper

____ waterless hand sanitizer

Personal Gear

____ toothbrush

____ toothpaste

____ dental floss

____ comb

____ hair brush

____ hair bands or ties

____ personal hygiene items

____ biodegradable soap and/or shampoo

____ washcloth or bandanna

____ pack towel

____ nail clippers

____ plastic washtub

SLEEP GEAR CHECKLIST

____ 2 sets pajamas
____ warm hat
____ sleeping bag, baby bag, or webbing to make youth sleeping bag shorter
____ fleece snowsuit, baby bag, or bag doubler for infants
____ sleep pad
____ camp pillow
____ favorite blanket
____ travel bed rail or child gate (optional)
____ backpacking chair (optional)

SAFETY CHECKLISTS

Basic Gear

____ bike or other helmets
____ bear bells, bear spray
____ repair kits (tires, pins, etc., for equipment)
____ whistle, mirror, or other signaling device
____ cell phone

First-aid Kit

____ children's and/or infant aspirin
____ children's antihistamine such as Benadryl (check with pediatrician first)
____ calamine lotion or other anti-itch cream
____ homeopathics such as arnica gel
____ antibiotic ointment
____ children's antibiotics (for extended trip)
____ adhesive bandages in varied sizes
____ tweezers, scissors
____ tape, gauze pads and/or dressings
____ pocket-sized first-aid guide
____ prescription medications

CHILD-TRANSPORTING GEAR CHECKLIST

____ soft child carrier (Baby Bjorn, sling, or wrap)
____ frame baby backpack
____ jogging stroller or bike trailer
____ mirror to check on riders behind you

CAMPING CHECKLISTS

Basic Gear

____ tent (optional: multiroomed)

____ ground cloth

____ stakes (bring extra)

____ mat or blanket for children to sit and/or play on

____ screen tent

____ pup tent or portable playpen with netting

____ beach umbrella

____ tarp

____ rope or line to tie off tarp

____ camp chairs

____ booster chairs

____ portable folding tables

____ coolers

____ parachute cord (for clothesline)

____ clothespins

____ whisk broom

____ doormat

____ camp stove, fuel

____ firewood, kindling

____ lighter, matches, firestarter

____ flashlight, headlamp

Miscellaneous Gear

____ laundry basket

____ light sticks (these glow for several hours when you crack the middle; can be worn around the neck or wrist or attached to clothing)

____ duct tape (wrap a long strip around trekking poles for easy storage)

____ trekking poles

____ camera, extra batteries, extra memory stick

BOATING CHECKLIST

____ personal flotation device (PFD)
____ whistle
____ throw rope
____ canoe, kayak, sailboat, raft
____ paddles
____ pump
____ repair kit
____ bilge towel
____ bilge bucket
____ water shoes, rain boots, or sandals
____ paddling gloves
____ dry bags
____ sewing kit
____ fishing rods and gear (optional)

PLAY AND NATURE ACTIVITIES CHECKLIST

____ bucket and shovel
____ stacking cups
____ infant toys and links
____ 1 stuffed animal (if child is attached to it)
____ disposable camera or cheap digital camera
____ water toys
____ magnifying glass
____ sidewalk chalk
____ small kid-sized day pack
____ harmonica, guitar, bells, etc.
____ colored pencils, waterproof notepad
____ cheap binoculars
____ bug jar, bug net
____ ball, flying disk
____ kite
____ playing cards, dice
____ Scrabble tiles (not the board)
____ Fundanas games
____ guidebooks, field guides

FOOD CHECKLISTS
D=Day Trip | C=Car Camping | B=Base Camping | P=Paddle Sports | S=Sailing | BP=Backpacking

COOKING EQUIPMENT	D	C	B	P	S	BP
two-burner camp stove and fuel	x	x		x		
backpacking stove and fuel	x	x	x	x	x	
firewood and kindling	x	x				
lighter, matches, flint stick	x	x	x	x	x	
fire starter	x	x	x	x		
large two-quart cookpot	x	x				
medium-sized one-quart cookpot	x	x	x	x	x	
small half-quart cookpot	x	x	x	x	x	x
fry pan	x	x			x	
flat pan or griddle	x	x			x	
dutch oven	x	x				
outback baker	x	x	x	x	x	x
aluminum foil	x	x		x	x	
pot holder	x	x	x	x	x	x
large stirring spoon	x	x			x	
spatula	x	x			x	
tongs	x	x			x	
long-handled forks for marshmallows, hot dogs	x	x			x	x
KITCHEN EQUIPMENT	**D**	**C**	**B**	**P**	**S**	**BP**
shade tarp	x	x		x		
screen tent large enough for picnic table	x	x				
screen tent to eat in	x	x		x		
folding table	x	x				
camp chairs	x	x				
clamp-on high chair or booster seat	x	x			x	
tablecloth and clips to hold it in place	x	x				
cooler and ice	x	x			x	
cutting mat	x	x	x	x	x	x
large cutting knife	x	x			x	
folding knife	x	x	x	x	x	x
hand-cranked baby-food grinder	x	x			x	
large serving and/or mixing bowl	x	x			x	

D=Day Trip | C=Car Camping | B=Base Camping | P=Paddle Sports | S=Sailing | BP=Backpacking

KITCHEN EQUIPMENT, cont.	D	C	B	P	S	BP
medium-sized serving and/or mixing bowl	x	x			x	
egg container and/or banana case	x	x		x	x	
five-gallon water jug, preferably with spout	x	x				
water purifying system or filter	x	x	x	x	x	x
one- or two-quart thermos	x	x		x	x	x
coffee press	x	x	x	x	x	
can opener	x	x		x	x	
bottle opener	x	x		x	x	
gallon-size resealable plastic bags	x	x	x	x	x	x
sandwich-size resealable plastic bags	x	x			x	x
CLEANING EQUIPMENT	**D**	**C**	**B**	**P**	**S**	**BP**
large trash bags	x	x			x	
paper towels	x	x			x	
sponge, dish scrubber	x	x		x	x	
bottle brush						
biodegradable liquid soap	x	x	x	x	x	
disposal wipes	x	x	x	x	x	x
hand sanitizer	x	x	x	x	x	x
large washtub or bucket for bathing or dishes	x	x			x	
small wash bin or bucket for hand washing	x	x				
EATING UTENSILS	**D**	**C**	**B**	**P**	**S**	**BP**
mugs for hot drinks	x	x	x	x	x	x
sippy cups	x	x	x	x	x	x
water bottles	x	x	x	x	x	x
water bladders	x	x	x	x	x	x
spoons, forks	x	x	x	x	x	x
bibs	x	x	x	x	x	x
plates	x	x			x	
bowls	x	x	x	x	x	
paper plates and bowls	x	x				
baby bottles, nipples, caps	x	x	x	x	x	x
baby spoon	x	x	x	x	x	x

INDEX

ACKNOWLEDGMENTS

Many thanks to my amazing children, who gave me the inspiration and reason to write this book; without them, it never would have happened. Great thanks to my husband and his always-encouraging words. Thanks to many patient friends who helped with so many edits. And thanks to my parents, who taught me to stop and appreciate the little things. Finally, thanks to the hundreds of families who asked questions, shared stories and pictures, and discovered the joy of bringing babies into wild places.

Special thanks to the following families for sharing their pictures: Andersons, Balls, Banks, Barkers, Basksis, Bauders, Boyds, Brauns, Brocks, Capuozos, Dittos, Donovans, Eldridges, Finemans, Fontanas, Gaulkes, Gordons, Grantiers, Grossheuschs, Hanleys, Hinshaws, Hodgsons, Hoggards, Hugheses, Keelers, MacFarlanes, Matermans, McGees, Michaels, Millers, Olivers, Rocks, Rufners, Rybickis, Schnells, Stevens, Swansons, Thomases, Twiggs, Wagners, and Wright-Elsons. You are all awesome families!.

ABOUT THE AUTHOR

JENNIFER AIST has been taking her four children into the backcountry since they were each newborns. She is passionate about exploring, discovering, and connecting children with nature. As a family, the Aists have logged hundreds of miles on trails, rivers, and oceans. Jennifer and her husband both volunteer for Alaska Search and Rescue Dogs and are active members of the outdoors community in Alaska. Jennifer is the director of parent education and a lactation consultant at Providence Children's Hospital in Anchorage, Alaska, where she teaches Babes in the Woods, Babes in the Snow, and Babes on the Water classes each year.

The author with her husband, their four children, and the family dogs. [JEN AIST]

ABOUT THE CONTRIBUTORS

KENDRA TWIGG grew up in the Pacific Northwest and settled in Alaska after attending college in the Land of the Midnight Sun. She became a part owner in an adventure travel–tour business and was involved in meal planning and packing for extended kayak tours, eventually also guiding the trips and preparing the meals in the field. Currently residing in Kingston, Washington, with her husband and two children, Kendra is passionate about providing healthy, tasty meals for her family . . . both at home and in camp.

JANE HODGSON, a physiotherapist in Yorkshire, England, specializes in lower-body injuries. She has competed in running, orienteering, and adventure racing. She also regularly takes her two children canoeing, sailing, rock climbing, backpacking, orienteering, geocaching, and cross-country running. The Backpacking chapter includes her sage advice about packing, lifting, and wearing a backpack.

THE MOUNTAINEERS, founded in 1906, is a nonprofit outdoor activity and conservation club, whose mission is "to explore, study, preserve, and enjoy the natural beauty of the outdoors. . . ." Based in Seattle, Washington, the club is now one of the largest such organizations in the United States, with seven branches throughout Washington State.

The Mountaineers sponsors both classes and year-round outdoor activities in the Pacific Northwest, which include hiking, mountain climbing, ski-touring, snowshoeing, bicycling, camping, canoeing and kayaking, nature study, sailing, and adventure travel. The club's conservation division supports environmental causes through educational activities, sponsoring legislation, and presenting informational programs.

All club activities are led by skilled, experienced volunteers, who are dedicated to promoting safe and responsible enjoyment and preservation of the outdoors.

If you would like to participate in these organized outdoor activities or the club's programs, consider a membership in The Mountaineers. For information and an application, write or call The Mountaineers, Club Headquarters, 7700 Sand Point Way NE, Seattle, WA 98115; 206-521-6001. You can also visit the club's website at www.mountaineers.org or contact The Mountaineers via email at clubmail@mountaineers.org.

The Mountaineers Books, an active, nonprofit publishing program of the club, produces guidebooks, instructional texts, historical works, natural history guides, and works on environmental conservation. All books produced by The Mountaineers Books fulfill the club's mission. Visit www.mountaineersbooks.org to find details about all our titles and the latest author events, as well as videos, web clips, links, and more!

The Mountaineers Books
1001 SW Klickitat Way, Suite 201
Seattle, WA 98134
800-553-4453
mbooks@mountaineersbooks.org

The Mountaineers Books is proud to be a corporate sponsor of The Leave No Trace Center for Outdoor Ethics, whose mission is to promote and inspire responsible outdoor recreation through education, research, and partnerships. The Leave No Trace program is focused specifically on human-powered (nonmotorized) recreation.
Leave No Trace strives to educate visitors about the nature of their recreational impacts, as well as offer techniques to prevent and minimize such impacts. Leave No Trace is best understood as an educational and ethical program, not as a set of rules and regulations.
For more information, visit www.lnt.org, or call 800-332-4100.